Essential
Property Investment
Calculations

Also by the author

Property Investment for Beginners
Robert Heaton

Essential Property Investment Calculations
Robert Heaton

The Property Investment Playbook – Volume 1
Robert Heaton & Ye Feng

The Property Investment Playbook – Volume 2
Robert Heaton & Ye Feng

Essential Property Investment Calculations

The numbers led approach to property investment and property management

Robert Heaton

Get the free resources

I've prepared some free resources to accompany the material in this book. All you need to do to access them is register for free on my website. These resources include the following:

- my spreadsheet for assessing property deals
- my spreadsheet for modelling a property refurbishment
- a one-page summary of all the key calculations

The spreadsheets are the ones I use myself for assessing buy-to-let property deals. It's all completely free with no sell on. Just sign up at my website at:

www.essentialproperty.net/free-resources

Contents

Introduction

Ever since I was young I've been fascinated by numbers. Numbers and statistics have the power to explain the world around us. They can be used to predict the motion of the planets around our sun or the location of an electron around an atom. From the big to the small, the predictive power of mathematics is the bedrock of our modern world. Without it, we wouldn't have put a man on the moon (several men in fact) or invented the barcode scanner. And it's my fascination with numbers that led me to write this book.

When I first started investing in property several years ago, I'd been working as an actuary for over ten years. If you've never heard of an actuary, don't worry – only a few people have. Actuaries use mathematical techniques and models, taken from fields like statistics, economics and finance, to work on a wide range of business problems. In the insurance industry, for example, actuaries are involved in setting the price of your car insurance, a process that involves estimating the probability of the policyholder having an accident and the likely cost of the pay-out if they do. In areas like pensions, where I work, actuaries are involved in estimating the amount of money that companies need to set aside to pay peoples' pensions. This requires estimates of how long people will live, future rates of inflation (peoples' pensions are often linked to inflation) and views on the likely investment returns on different asset classes. For a pop culture portrayal of an actuary, you need look no further then Reuben Feffer (Ben Stiller's character) in the 2004 movie Along Came Polly.

When I first started out in property, I began by doing what any diligent actuarial student would do – I ordered lots of books from Amazon and I read them all. Before long, and with the help of a few choice podcasts I discovered along the way, I became well-versed in the language and legal aspects of property investment. I took my first step when I invested in a two-bedroom flat in Leeds city centre, an area I was familiar with having lived there for a number of years. And my property investment journey was underway.

It wasn't until several years and a handful of property investments later that I found my knowledge lacking in a few places. At first it was around questions like how to measure the returns I'd achieved on my property investments and on my portfolio as a whole and what I could do to improve this performance. Then later, it was around more fundamental questions like how the investment appraisal techniques commonly used by property investors marry up with some of the asset valuation techniques I'd learned in my formal actuarial training. As an actuary, valuation exercises are often carried out by estimating future cash flows and calculating their present value using discounted cash flow techniques. As a property investor, I was more used to thinking about rental yields, monthly cash flows, and my return on investment. I began to think more deeply about how these two views of the world came together and to ask myself if there was anything to be gained by applying my actuarial mindset to property investment.

What I discovered through my later research is that there's a huge gulf between the techniques used by individual investors in the residential buy-to-let market and the more disciplined, numbers-led approach used by professional real estate investment companies and institutional investors. Professional property investors, with bigger budgets and access to a range of specialists, use a wide range of mathematical techniques and formalised metrics to assess property deals and to manage their residential and commercial real estate portfolios. These techniques are lifted from a variety of places and passed down from expert to expert in the same way your grandma might pass down her famous chicken soup recipe. But there was no single source of knowledge or wisdom that brings all these calculation techniques and metrics together in one place.

I wrote this book to bridge that gap.

Essential Property Investment Calculations is a guide to all the calculations, numerical techniques, and metrics you need to know to take your property investing to the next level. If you're new to property investment, the book will teach you the calculations you need to know to put your property education on solid ground from day one. For experienced investors, I hope the book will challenge you to think about how you assess property deals and how you assess the performance of your investments over time. The book is split into two parts: the first part is all about assessing property deals; the second part is all about longer term portfolio management.

In Part One, we'll start out with the basic rental yield calculations, covering everything from gross yield to capitalisation rate, then we'll move on to stress testing deal cash flows and margin for safety. We'll cover a range of property valuation techniques you can use to value residential property. I'll put some of these valuation techniques on a more formal footing using language taken from the field of surveying. Finally, we'll look at all the calculations you need to know to secure financing for your property deal and at a range of negotiation tips and tricks you can use to get your deal over the line.

In Part Two, we'll start out with a crash course in accounting. This chapter lays the foundation for everything else that we'll cover in the second half of the book. I'll teach you how to measure property returns, both at the total portfolio level and on a property-by-property basis. Next, we'll look at a range of key performance indicators or KPIs that professional property investors use to assess the performance of their portfolio and to work out what's going wrong (or right) and the levers they can pull to improve performance. In the chapter on portfolio risk management, I'll apply some actuarial thinking to questions like how big a cash buffer do I need to hold to manage liquidity risk, and we'll take a look at how you can use scenario testing based on historical events like the Great Depression of the 1930s or the inflationary oil shock of the 1970s to resilience-test your portfolio. Finally, we'll look at my golden rules of portfolio building and how you can use the property cycle to build a better property portfolio faster.

Everything in this book is geared towards making you a better property investor by giving you access to a range of quantitative, mathematical techniques that took me years to refine. It's designed to take your thinking to the next level and to give you some formal frameworks to support you in your decision making. If numbers aren't your fascination just yet, my hope is that they will be by the end of this book. Most of all, I hope that you have fun reading this book and that it changes at least something about the way you look at deals and manage your property portfolio.

Part One

Assessing a property deal

Chapter 1

Rental yield calculations

An investment operation is one which, upon thorough analysis, promises safety of principal and an adequate return.

–Benjamin Graham, *The Intelligent Investor*

When it comes to assessing a property deal, the best place to start is rental yield. Rental yield calculations are at the heart of property investing, and a good understanding of these calculations and what goes into them is essential knowledge for every property investor. But what are the right calculations to use and what target returns should you be aiming for? In this chapter, we'll take a look at the most common rental yield calculations used by investors, how to carry out the calculations and when you should use them.

Let's start with gross yield

If you've spent any time at all around property-types, you'll have heard a lot of talk about yield. In fact, you might have picked up the impression that yield is the only thing that matters – we'll come back to that idea. But what is yield and how should you calculate it?

Let's start with gross yield. Gross yield is simply the annual rental income from a property divided by the purchase price of the property. So, for those of you who like a formula:

$$Gross\ yield = \frac{Annual\ rental\ income}{Purchase\ price}$$

Let's take a quick example. Suppose we're looking at property with an expected monthly rent of £500 and a purchase price of £100,000. We calculate the annual rental income as 12 × £500 = £6,000 and we divide by £100,000. This gives us a result of 0.06 – that is, a gross yield of 6% p.a. It's as simple as that.

You can, if you like, incorporate any additional purchase costs, for example stamp duty, legal expenses, survey costs and mortgage broker fees, into this gross yield calculation. To do this, you simply need to add these to the purchase price in the bottom of the formula above. In practice, most investors don't typically do this. We'll come onto why next.

Is gross yield useful?

So, it's simple to calculate, but what is it good for? (Spoiler alert: the answer isn't absolutely nothing.) Firstly, gross yield is a simple way to compare different investments. For example, all other things being equal, an investor would prefer a property that offered an 8% p.a. gross yield to one that offered 6% p.a. Secondly, you only need a small amount of information to calculate it. So, it's a quick and easy place to start when assessing potential property deals.

However, the limitation of gross yield is that it doesn't consider your upkeep costs. For example, it doesn't consider the likely difference in costs between houses and apartments – the latter will often have a service charge and ground rent. Furthermore, two houses, one a new build detached and one an old Victorian terrace, could have the same gross yield, but the repair costs for the older property will likely be much higher. Which of these two properties would you prefer to own?

In short, gross yield is quite a crude return metric. It's the one talked about most often by property investors and on popular UK TV shows like Homes Under the Hammer. But it's really only useful for headline comparisons and perhaps an initial screening of potential investments. This is why most investors don't bother to add in all the likely purchase costs in their gross yield calculation.

So if gross yield is only good up to a certain point, let's take a look at some other rental yield calculations that can give us a better picture of our likely investment returns.

Introducing net yield and capitalisation rate

For a more accurate picture of our return on investment, we need a more powerful yield metric. That's where net yield and capitalisation rate come in. Let's look at the calculation of net yield first.

Net yield explained

Net yield is the annual rental profit from the property divided by the purchase price of the property. Net yield is calculated as follows:

$$Net\ yield = \frac{Annual\ rental\ profit}{Purchase\ price}$$

or

$$Net\ yield = \frac{(Annual\ rental\ income - Annual\ rental\ costs)}{Purchase\ price}$$

Again, let's look at a quick example. Suppose we have annual rental income of £6,000, annual rental costs of £4,000, and a purchase price of £100,000. We calculate the annual rental profit as £6,000 – £4,000 = £2,000 and we divide by the purchase price of £100,000. This gives us a result of 0.02 – that is, we calculate a net yield of 2% p.a.

When calculating the net yield for a potential property investment, we need to include all the costs associated with running the property over the course of the year. For example, we would include all the following costs:

- mortgage payments

- marketing costs
- letting agent fees
- repair and maintenance costs
- service charges and ground rent
- insurance costs (e.g. buildings insurance)
- an allowance for voids (e.g. lost rent, utilities)
- other administration costs

That is, we need to include pretty much everything we can think of cost-wise in the calculation to give us the most accurate picture possible of our likely rental returns.

So is net yield any better than gross yield?

Net yield is a much better metric to use when comparing potential investments. It considers all the costs of running your rental property, so it's based on the money you'll have left over after all costs have been paid. Also, it shows up any fundamental differences in the running costs of different properties, e.g. between flats and houses, old and new properties, etc. That means it provides a much better comparison of the potential investment returns across different types of property.

At this point, you might be thinking that a 2% p.a. net yield doesn't sound very good, given you could probably get 0.5% p.a. in your bank account? And taken at face value, a 2% p.a. net return certainly doesn't sound enough to compensate you for the risks and hassle of starting and running a property business.

However, the key factor that net yield ignores is the amount of cash you have tied up in the investment. Net yield compares our annual rental profit with the purchase price of the property. But we're unlikely to have purchased the property in full, in cash – we're more likely to have used a mortgage, so we won't have put in 100% of the purchase price ourselves.

For this reason, there are a couple of other calculations we can use instead that are much better than net yield. The first of these is a calculation popular with US property investors. It's little used by individual buy-to-let investors in the UK, but it's commonly used by surveyors and big institutional investors. It's also at the heart of some of the valuation techniques we'll come on to in a later chapter. So, let's take a short trip over the pond.

Capitalisation rate explained

Closely related to net yield is the capitalisation rate or "cap rate" for a property. Much more widely used by US investors, cap rate is a variation on net yield that's arguably much more useful.

Let's look at how to calculate it. Cap rate is calculated as the annual net operating profit from the property divided by the purchase price of the property, assuming the investor buys the property in full without using a mortgage. As such, the calculation excludes mortgage costs. Capitalisation rate is calculated as follows:

$$Cap\ rate = \frac{Annual\ net\ operating\ profit}{Purchase\ price}$$

or

$$Cap\ rate = \frac{(Annual\ rental\ income - Annual\ rental\ costs)}{Purchase\ price}$$

So, the only difference between net yield and cap rate is that cap rate excludes mortgage costs. We still need to include all the other costs that we listed above, i.e. marketing costs, letting agent fees, repair costs, service charges, ground rent, insurance costs, etc.

Let's look at a quick example based on the same property as above. We have annual rental income of £6,000 and annual rental costs of £1,500 excluding mortgage costs. Our purchase price is still £100,000. We calculate the annual net operating profit as £6,000 – £1,500 = £4,500 and we divide by the purchase price of £100,000. This gives us a result of 0.045 – that is, a cap rate of 4.5% p.a.

Why is cap rate useful?

Cap rate is useful precisely because it excludes mortgage costs. The formula for cap rate is based solely on the profitability of the rental property itself, not on the mortgage financing used by the buyer to purchase the property.

In practice, different investors use different levels of deposit and have access to different mortgage financing options. Mortgage costs will, therefore, be different for each individual investor, and so two investors might come up with a different figure for net yield, even for the same property. But cap rate is not affected in the same way.

Because cap rate assumes that you buy a property in cash with no leverage or mortgage financing, it gives investors a measure of the rental returns they could expect if they owned the property outright and had no mortgage costs. It allows investors to compare potential property purchases on a consistent basis, leaving the financing decisions until later.

It's little used by individual buy-to-let property investors in the UK, but it's a metric you absolutely need to have in your toolkit. We'll return to cap rate again in a later chapter, so it's worth making sure you properly understand this calculation and what goes into it before you move on.

Return on investment ("ROI")

The second calculation we can use instead of net yield is return on investment or ROI. This calculation shows us how our rental profits compare with the actual cash we have invested in the deal.

Let's look at how to calculate it.

ROI is the annual rental profit from the property divided by the cash you've invested in the deal. If you bought a property in cash without a mortgage, this would be the same as the cap rate. But if you used a mortgage, you'll have put in much less of your own cash.

$$ROI = \frac{Annual\ rental\ profit}{Cash\ invested}$$

or

$$ROI = \frac{(Annual\ rental\ income - Annual\ rental\ costs)}{Cash\ invested}$$

Working with our previous example, we have a property with annual rental profits of £2,000 once we've subtracted out the mortgage costs again. We purchased the property for £100,000, but we borrowed 75% or £75,000 from the bank to buy it. That means we only put in £25,000 of our own cash.

Let's calculate our return on investment. We take the annual rental profit of £2,000 p.a. and we divide by £25,000. This gives us an answer of 0.08 – that is, an ROI of 8% p.a. Now that's sounding more like it – worth getting out of bed for.

In practice, we also need to consider additional costs like stamp duty, legal expenses, surveys, broker fees, etc. These are all real cash costs that need to be paid upfront, and so we should add all of these to the "cash invested" in our ROI formulae above.

What does ROI tell us?

ROI is our best guess at the return we're actually going to achieve on our cash. Because of this, you can even compare it with the returns you'd get on non-property investments, e.g. the interest that we'd receive on a bank account or the dividend yield on a share. It shows you how hard your money is working for you and how this compares with other available investments.

Which of these calculations is the best?

All the calculations we've looked at so far have their uses. Here's a summary of the main pros of each one.

- Gross yield is quick and simple and it's okay for comparing investments when they have similar running costs
- Cap rate estimates the return you'd achieve if you owned the property outright and separates out the financing decision, so it gives a more objective measure of the potential returns
- Return on investment shows you how hard your money is working for you

For most investors, ROI is the most useful of these calculations. It factors in all the running costs of the investment and it takes into account the method you're using to finance the deal. It also tells us something about the likely payback period for the investment.

Let's take our previous example again. With an ROI of 8% p.a. we can expect our investment to pay us back in 12.5 years. That is, if it pays us back 8% of the cash invested each year, then in 12.5 years it will have paid us back 100% of the cash we invested.

$$Payback\ period = \frac{1}{ROI}$$

Payback period is a useful concept in investing. It tells us the length of time we'd need to hold the investment for it to pay us back the money we've invested. It follows that if we don't think the investment is going to be profitable for at least that length of time, we should give this investment a miss.

In summary, gross yield is useful for screening potential investments in the early stages of due diligence. Cap rate is useful for comparisons between properties and for property valuation work, which we'll come back to in Chapter 3. But ROI is the ultimate metric, and it's the one you'll likely base most of your investment decisions on. In all honesty, most investors don't use net yield at all.

What about capital growth?

So far, all the calculations we've looked at only consider rental income. But for many investors, capital growth is the reason they invest in property. So how do we factor this in?

Capital growth is the uplift in the value of a property over time. It's often said that in property, the real money is made through capital growth. And whilst that might well be true, the level of capital growth you can expect is inherently uncertain, as is the timeframe over which this growth will play out. No-one knows how the future will play out, and if they say they do they're probably just after your money.

Having said all that, when it comes to capital growth, are there any trends from the past that we might use as a guide to the future?

Learning from the past

Robert Shiller's study, summarised in his famous book *Irrational Exuberance*, shows that over much of the 20th century, property prices in the US pretty much tracked price inflation. At best, depending on the timeframe chosen, property prices tracked around inflation plus 0.5% p.a. Comparable studies of UK property prices have come to very similar conclusions.

What these studies also show, however, is that capital growth is far from a straight line. There are periods when property prices have risen dramatically, times when they've fallen, and other times where they've just pottered along. There are big regional variations hiding under the surface, adding further complexity. There are even street-by-street variations in the same city.

For these reasons, most property investors exclude capital growth from their calculations when they assess a deal. However, investors will often change the criteria they use for accepting or rejecting a deal depending on how they feel about the capital growth prospects and the riskiness (or not) of a particular investment. So, although capital growth doesn't feature explicitly in the rental yield calculations, it can be factored into the decision-making process overall.

Let's take a closer look at how this works.

What's a good rental yield for buy-to-let?

Which property would you buy from the following? Property No. 1 has an 8% p.a. ROI and is located in a nice family neighbourhood in a local commuter town. Property No. 2 has a lower 5% p.a. ROI, but it's located in a city centre and has strong capital growth potential.

With property investment decisions, there are sometimes no clear-cut choices. A good ROI or capitalisation rate will depend on your personal investment criteria and your preferences. It will also depend on your views and convictions around the future of a property and its location.

In practice, many investors are prepared to accept a lower ROI and capitalisation rate if they expect a particular property or location will achieve stronger capital growth in the future. To illustrate this point, the table below shows the minimum rental yield a property investor might accept on a residential buy-to-let in the UK right now. It shows how the investor might flex their investment criteria (i.e. the cap rate or ROI they're prepared to accept) depending on their views on the capital growth potential for a property.

How an investor might flex their investment criteria

Growth potential	High	Medium	Low
Gross yield	6% – 8% p.a.	7% – 9% p.a.	8% – 10% p.a.
Cap rate	4.0% – 5.0% p.a.	4.5% – 5.5% p.a.	5.0% – 6.0% p.a.
ROI	5% – 8% p.a.	7% – 10% p.a.	9% – 12% p.a.

For example, say you feel confident that the property price and the market rent for a property in central Manchester will continue to grow for years to come. You may choose to accept an ROI of 5% p.a. today, even though there are higher yielding investment opportunities out there. You wouldn't be alone in this decision, and there are many investors who would do the same.

In short, you can flex the criteria you apply to these rental yield calculations, depending on your views around the future growth prospects for a property and for an area.

Finding an approach that works for you

For me personally, I don't like following an investment strategy that depends on speculation to succeed. It could be smart speculation, but it's still speculation. And the amount and timing of any future capital growth are still just educated guesses. Because of this, I like to go for properties that are a bit more in the middle – that is, they have a good ROI and a reasonable chance of growth over the long term.

That being said, it's all about your personal goals and objectives. You'll have to decide what's most important to you.

Finally, I need to add a quick caveat about the above table and numbers. This table is based on my investment criteria as of early 2020 for buy-to-let investments in the UK. What constitutes a good rental yield varies throughout the property cycle. Yields are often highest after a property crash and lowest in the boom period. Also, different investors include different costs in their modelling, with some investors including the cost of every last gas safety check and others taking a less detailed approach. What matters most is that you are comfortable with your own criteria and that you keep your calculation approach consistent between properties.

Using rental yield calculations to set your price

We can use the rental yield calculations above to set the maximum price that we're prepared to pay for a property.

For example, suppose we've decided that a particular property needs to achieve an ROI of 6% p.a. to get us interested in doing a deal. We can play around with the price in our calculation spreadsheet until the ROI equals 6% p.a. This price is then the maximum price we're prepared to pay. If you don't have a deal calculation spreadsheet, I'll send you my spreadsheet for free – details on how to get hold of your copy are provided at the end of the book.

There's no guarantee that the seller will be interested in selling to us at that price, of course. But this technique can help us to set our walk-away point before we enter negotiations. We'll develop this idea much more fully and formally in a later chapter on how to value residential property.

Finally, a word about tax.

It's worth clarifying that all the rental yield calculations discussed in this chapter are calculations before tax is applied. So, if you calculate an ROI of 8% p.a. based on the formula above, then your actual returns will be less than that after tax.

You should take the time to understand how tax will impact your investments. How you set your business up from a tax perspective is extremely important. However, I've not considered this further here, because tax calculations depend on your personal circumstances and can quickly get very complicated.

If you need to know more about the tax aspects of property investment and about the best way to set up your portfolio, then please do speak to an accountant or a tax adviser about the right legal structure and set up for your property business.

In conclusion

You're now officially an expert in rental yield calculations and you've upped your property pub chat leaps and bounds. You'll even be able to chat to US real estate guys about cap rates.

In all seriousness, the rental yield calculations we've covered here will quickly become your best friends. They will help you assess and compare property deals, force you to define the returns you'll accept, and give you plenty of chat for those all-important property networking events. All in all, not a bad start.

Payback period, the reciprocal of ROI, is also a useful Jedi mind trick. It can help focus your mind on the longer-term prospects for an investment and help you rule out certain properties.

You can and should have different criteria for accepting and rejecting deals, based on your convictions about future capital growth potential. Where the capital growth prospects appear less strong, you absolutely should demand a higher ROI or cap rate from your property investment.

Finally, it's worthwhile saying that the number one criteria for accepting or rejecting a deal is that it should be cash flow positive. Since this is such an important concept, we've dedicated our next chapter entirely to this topic.

Chapter 2

Stress testing deal cash flow

After all, you only find out who is swimming naked when the tide goes out.

–Warren Buffet, *Berkshire Hathaway Annual Report*

Anyone who's read Rich Dad Poor Dad by Robert Kiyosaki will understand the importance of making investments that provide a positive cash flow. For those who haven't read the book, here's a quick question. How many properties can you own if each one is cash flow negative and costs you £200 per month out of your own pocket to meet the monthly expenses? The answer (not a hard one) is probably not that many at all.

In this chapter, we're going to look at the most important idea in property investment – cash flow. We'll look at how to calculate cash flow, how to stress test a potential deal and what actions you can take to improve your monthly cash flow. We'll also take a look at a concept from stock investing, known as margin for safety, and see how we might apply this idea to our property deals and to our cash flow calculations. There's lots to cover here, so let's get started.

An introduction to cash flow

Property investors love to talk about cash flow. Cash flow is simply the cash profit the property makes each month or year after all expenses are taken into account.

It's closely related to ROI, which we looked at in the last chapter. We can calculate cash flow on an annual basis using the following formula:

$$Cash\ flow = (Annual\ rental\ income - Annual\ rental\ costs)$$

or on a monthly basis

$$Cash\ flow = \frac{(Annual\ rental\ income - Annual\ rental\ costs)}{12}$$

A cash flow positive property then is simply one that gives a positive number for either of the two formulae above. It's an investment that puts cash in your back pocket each month, rather than one which costs you money each month.

I like to work with monthly cash flows, as I've set myself an income target per month from my property investments, and I'm working towards that monthly income goal as I build my portfolio. But it's really up to you which number you prefer.

As an example, suppose we're looking at a potential property deal where the annual rental income is expected to be £6,000 and annual rental costs have been estimated at £3,600. We calculate the annual cash flow as £6,000 – £3,600 = £2,400 and we divide by 12. This gives us a cash flow of £200 per month. So, based on our modelling and the assumptions we've made about the rental income and rental expenses, we expect the investment to put £200 in our back pocket each month. Not too shabby, eh?

The cash flow frown

Real life cash flows are unlikely to be as smooth and consistent as £200 per month. There could be months when cash flow is zero or potentially even negative. Our cash flow estimate above is simply a guess at the average cash flow per month, assuming cash flows are spread out evenly across the whole year. But if real life cash flows aren't smooth, then what shape are they? Well, they're shaped a bit like a frown.

Rental expenses are often higher at the start of a tenancy. You'll be paying for things like advertising the property to potential tenants, final repairs, inventory checks, and so on. Likewise, at the end of a tenancy, there will be higher costs related to cleaning, refurbishment, and tenant check-outs. Rental costs in the middle of a tenancy will likely be lower, but with some lumps and bumps along the way due to one-off repairs, service charges, ground rents, etc. But our rental income, the other side of the cash flow equation, will likely be spread evenly throughout the tenancy.

In general, you won't go far wrong if you expect your cash flows to be frown-shaped – lower at the start and end of a tenancy and higher in the middle. This means you'll likely need some cash in your account at the start of a tenancy to meet any initial upfront costs. You'll also need some funds spare at the end of the tenancy, so don't take out all the cash you make in the middle.

Knowing what you can expect around the timing of cash flows across the tenancy as a whole will hopefully turn your cash flow frown, upside down. It's also worth pointing out that as the number of properties in your portfolio starts to growth, the monthly cash flows will likely smooth themselves out to some extent, as not all your tenancies will start and end at the same time.

Why is cash flow important?

When it comes to surviving a property crash, cash flow is king. In fact, it was a lack of focus on cash flow that got many investors into trouble in the 2007-2008 financial crisis. With property prices soaring, these investors were caught up in the mania of the property boom and didn't pay close enough attention to cash flow. We'll come back to what I dub the "capital growth trap" later in this chapter.

To see why cash flow is so important, it's worth looking at how investors typically go bust. Firstly, investors get themselves into a situation where their whole portfolio is cash flow negative. This could happen due to higher than expected rental expenses or a rise in interest rates and mortgage costs. The investor is then forced to subsidise their portfolio with cash from other earnings. When they can no longer meet their expenses, they're forced to sell quickly and often at rock bottom prices to avoid a repossession. If the sale price they achieve is greater than the outstanding mortgage balance, then the investor survives – for now. But if the sale price doesn't cover the mortgage balance, it can lead to a repossession and ultimately to bankruptcy.

The key to staying out of trouble then is to avoid making deals that are cash flow negative in the first place. So, let's take a closer look at what you can do about this.

How to get cash flow modelling right

The best thing we can do to avoid bad property deals is to improve the accuracy of our cash flow modelling. When estimating the future cash flows, we need good estimates of all the costs involved in running the property. We also need a good estimate of the potential future rental income from the property.

In practice, all the calculation work or 'modelling' is usually done on a simple spreadsheet. The whole process is a lot less onerous than it might sound from the detailed explanation below. Once your spreadsheet is set up, the modelling work amounts to inputting a few different numbers in your spreadsheet, and the hard part is doing the thinking behind those numbers in the first place.

With that in mind, let's take a closer look at each of the cash flows you'll be modelling and how to approach each of these estimates.

Rental income

The figure you use in the modelling should be a conservative estimate of the likely rental income from the property. Err on the side of caution. For example, if similar properties are being rented out for £675 to £725 per month right now in the market, go with the £675 figure. Also, you can speak to a letting agent in the local market to get their view on the potential rental income.

Mortgage interest

To get to grips with your likely mortgage costs, get in touch with your broker. When I'm modelling a deal, I always work off actual mortgage rates available at that time. If you're going to finance the deal using a 75% mortgage via a limited company, then you should use mortgage rates that are relevant to this situation.

Marketing and tenancy set-up costs

How you model these costs will depend on whether you intend to self-manage or use a letting agent. I like to use letting agents, so I try to include all the potential costs that I will be charged.

Since the tenant fees ban came into force last year, letting agents are increasingly pushing tenancy set-up costs on to landlords. Typical fees that you might encounter and an indicative cost figure you could use in your modelling are as follows:

- Marketing the property, e.g. £360
- Tenant reference checks, e.g. £120
- Preparing an inventory, e.g. £60
- Deposit registration, e.g. £60
- Tenancy renewals, e.g. £120

All-in, you're probably looking at a cost of around £600 in a year with a new tenancy set-up. Costs in a renewal year (where the tenant decides to stay) could be say £120. If the tenant stays for two years, these might average out at around £360 per year across the two years, so this might not be a bad figure to use in your cost modelling. Feel free to use your own estimates or refine my estimates above based on the likely costs in the area you're going to invest.

My main message here is not to underestimate these costs. Make sure you base your modelling on research of the actual costs of using local letting agents in the area.

Management fees

If you use a letting agent to manage your properties, you'll need to factor in this cost too. Management fees for a typical buy-to-let will be in the region of 10% to 12% of the monthly rent.

Repairs and maintenance

The cost of repairs and maintenance can vary a lot from property to property. Repair costs for a new build apartment might be close to zero. But maintenance costs for a three-bedroom Victorian terrace will likely be much higher. Also, with apartments, there will be a service charge that you'll need to factor in.

As a general rule of thumb, I tend to make an allowance of 0% to 5% of the monthly rent for apartments. I'd use something at the lower end of this range for a new build apartment. For houses, I typically make an allowance of 5% to 10% of the monthly rent, possibly higher for older houses with extensive maintenance issues.

Again, it's important to be consistent in your modelling and to err on the side of caution. Try not to underestimate these costs.

Service charges and ground rent

For leasehold apartments, there will typically be a service charge to cover maintenance for the building as a whole and ground rent payable to the freeholder. You should ask the estate agent for details of the latest charges when you're modelling a deal. You should also ask to see a copy of the lease. This will help you uncover any onerous clauses, e.g. around future increases in the ground rent.

Personally, when I've got my cash flow modelling wrong in the past, it's been because I've underestimated things like service charges. Try to find out as much as you can about the block, the current management company and whether these charges are likely to increase. If you can't find any information on this, try phoning a different estate agent in the same city or perhaps even the management company themselves. Err on the side of caution and consider increasing the cost you use in your modelling by 5% or 10% as a buffer against future adverse experience.

Insurance

For apartments, buildings insurance is sometimes included in the service charge. Sometimes it's not. Ask the estate agent – they often won't know the answer, but they can find this out for you. For houses, try phoning an insurance broker to ask for a quote or ask the seller for details about the cost of their building's insurance.

Factor in something small for public liability insurance and accidental damage cover. £60 to £90 per annum ought to do it.

Allowance for voids

In between tenancies, your property will likely be sitting idle for a couple of weeks. You should factor the cost of this into your cash flow estimates. I typically assume a void period of one month every two years, so I make an allowance for voids of two weeks per year in lost rental income.

There may be other costs you want to factor in here too. For example, the local council might charge council tax while the property is unoccupied – some do, some don't. Also, you'll need to cover the cost of any utilities used in the void period, e.g. electricity costs.

Other administration and compliance costs

There will be other smaller costs relating to administration and compliance. These will include things like gas safety checks, electrical safety testing, freeholder notification fees, plus others. I try to cost these out as accurately as I can, but some people just add in a lump sum to cover them off more generally. For example, you could add in £300 per annum. It's up to you how granular you want to go. I go with the policy of no surprises, so I tend to err on the side of more detail is better.

Finally, when vetting potential investments, it's important to be consistent. Don't include a gas safety check for one property and not another (unless there's no gas for that property). Consistency is important to ensure you make the right investment decisions and that the property you end up buying is the best deal you can do out of all the deals that cross your desk.

A word of caution on modelling

Looking at the list above, some property investors would think I'm crazy going to this level of detail. However, in my experience, this exercise is one of the most important things you can do to make better investment decisions. Many investors' modelling is extremely thin on costs and they're seriously undercooking the day-to-day running costs of their properties.

Although I know the costs I'm using in my modelling will turn out to be wrong, I try not to miss any key buckets of cost. So, even if the amounts aren't spot on, they'll be close enough that my modelling gives me a realistic idea of the returns I can expect.

Some investors, particularly new investors, are so keen to do a deal that they talk themselves into using increasingly optimistic cost assumptions. They do this to justify a higher purchase price and to increase the chances they'll close on a deal. If you find yourself doing this, bring it back to basics and try to come up with a prudent estimate based on your best guess at the likely costs involved. Better still, ask another experienced investor to review your modelling and your cost assumptions. If a deal doesn't work on fairly cautious assumptions, it's probably not worth doing anyway.

Margin for safety

So that's the initial cash flow modelling sorted. But how do we ensure that our property investments will work out to be cash flow positive all the time? To achieve this, we need to build a margin for safety into our calculations.

Margin for safety is a concept taken from the accounting world. In accounting, it's the amount that the sales or revenues of a business can drop before it starts to make a loss. It's a buffer, if you like, against future uncertainty. The concept was popularised in the investment world by Benjamin Graham, the famous value investor, in his highly popular book The Intelligent Investor.

Graham argues that sound investment decisions should build in a margin for safety. For him, this meant buying the investment at a discount to its "intrinsic value" – that is, at a price lower than what the stock was worth based on its earnings and growth prospects.

We're going to look at how we can use the margin for safety concept and apply it to our property investments to guarantee that we're making cash flow positive investments 100% of the time.

How to stress test a deal

So far, our modelling has got us to a sensible estimate of the monthly cash flow we can expect from a deal. This is our 'base case' – it's what we hope to achieve if everything works out as planned. However, we want to make sure that our investment is cash flow positive under a range of different scenarios. That's where stress testing comes in.

To stress test my cash flows, I look at the impact on monthly cash flows of an adverse change in one of my key assumptions. I first examine the impact on an "all other things being equal" basis – that is, I change just one assumption at a time. Then finally, I think about the potential combined impact of these changes.

You should aim to invest in deals where the cash flow is strong and where you expect it to remain positive under the combined impact of two or more stresses. That way, you're almost guaranteed to be doing a deal which is cash flow positive and which puts money in your pocket every month. So what changes in the assumptions should we consider in our stress testing?

(1) A fall in the market rent

You should consider the impact of a fall in market rent. This scenario could be relevant if there's a dip in local rents in the area, e.g. due to an oversupply of properties or a fall in tenant demand. It could also be relevant if there's a wider economic downturn which affects the entire rental sector.

So how much of a fall should we model? Well, following the 2007-2008 financial crisis, there was a fall in rents across most regions of the UK of around 2-3% p.a. for 12 to 18 months. As such, a sensible stress test might be a 5% fall in the monthly rental income from the property.

(2) An increase in mortgage interest costs

Mortgage costs will likely be your single largest expense. To stress test a deal, consider using a higher interest rate in your modelling. For example, you might be planning to borrow on a five-year fixed rate mortgage product where the initial rate of 3.5% p.a. reverts to 5% p.a. after five years. You could re-run your modelling based on the higher 5% p.a. rate and look at the impact on cash flow.

Average mortgage interest rates in the UK over the last 50 years have been much higher than this, so you could also consider a more pessimistic scenario based on say a 7% p.a. interest rate or higher.

(3) An increase in the service charge

For flats and apartments, the other big chunk of cost is usually the service charge. Service charges can be quite volatile, and they only tend to drift one way. A sensible stress test might be to assume a 10% or 20% increase in the annual service charge.

(4) An increase in repair costs

We've already looked at a typical allowance for repairs above – that is, 0% to 5% of the monthly rent for apartments and 5% to 10% of the rent for houses. In your stress test, you could consider increasing this allowance by say 5% from the figure you've used in your base case.

(5) A general increase in other costs

Finally, there will be a whole load of other costs which individually aren't that significant, but which can add up. It's not worth stress testing these costs individually, but you can group them together and consider say a 10% increase in the total.

Let's look at a real-life example

A few years ago, I purchased a one-bedroom flat in a city centre in the Northern Powerhouse. I purchased the flat for £120,000. In my base case, I was expecting a monthly rent of £750 and a net cash flow per month of £200. My expected expenses each month were £263 on the mortgage, £75 on the service costs and £212 on all other costs.

From a cash flow perspective, my margin for safety against future adverse changes was £200 per month. My stress testing was all based on this figure. And I looked at how the monthly cash flow would drop as each of my key assumptions changed.

Let's take a quick look at the results of the stress testing I carried out at the time. The impact shown in the table below is the reduction in the monthly cash flow as a result of the stress tests I applied.

The impact of various stress tests on monthly cash flow

Stress test	Cash flow impact / £
(1) A fall of 5% in the market rent *Calculation: £750 rent × 5%*	(38)
(2) Mortgage rate increase from 3.5% to 5.0% p.a. *Calculation: £263 monthly cost × 5.0% ÷ 3.5% – £263*	(113)
(3) An increase of 20% in the service charge *Calculation: (£900 annual service charge × 20%) ÷ 12*	(15)
(4) An increase in repairs from 0% to 5% of the rent *Calculation: £750 rent × 5%*	(38)
(5) An increase of 10% in all the other costs *Calculation: £210 per month (all other costs) × 10%*	(21)
Total impact	(225)

Based on the results of my stress testing, you can see that if all these changes were to play out at the same time, it would wipe out my margin for safety and leave me marginally cash flow negative. Let me explain. Under my base case, I was expecting a net cash flow of £200 per month. However, the combined impact of these five stress tests was a fall in monthly cash flow of £225. So, if all these things happened together, my net cash flow would fall to −£25 per month.

In practice, if we've built up our base case prudently, all these changes are unlikely to happen at once. In the case above, I concluded that the margin for safety was big enough and I was likely to end up with a positive cash flow in most foreseeable situations. If your stress testing comes to a different conclusion, e.g. that your cash flow has a high chance of turning negative, you might decide the margin for safety in that deal isn't large enough and that there's not enough of an investment case for that property.

Finally, this type of analysis can also be useful for thinking about the actions we can take to lower our risk and protect our cash flow position. For example, by taking out a fixed rate mortgage of five years or more, we can reduce our interest rate risk and lock in some of our costs in advance, thereby reducing the chance of a negative cash flow position in the future.

In conclusion

In this chapter, we've learned all about cash flow. We've looked at how to calculate it and how to improve our modelling. We've also learned about margin for safety and how to stress test a deal to make sure the investment is cash flow positive in the best and worst of times.

As a parting thought, it's worth calling out the two main reasons that property investments turn out to be cash flow negative for some property investors.

(1)   The capital growth trap – Investors chasing price growth will sometimes convince themselves it's okay to have thin margins for safety. They'll trade off yield and cash flow for the hope of capital growth – that's what I call the capital growth trap. The value investor, however, looks for a strong margin for safety and some growth potential, seeing growth potential and cash flow as two sides of the same deal.

(2)   Using too much leverage – The larger the amount of money you borrow, the thinner your margin for safety. If you're uncomfortable with the cash flow position, you could consider putting more money into the deal and borrowing less. It will lower your ROI but improve your cash flow position. Remember that debt is always destabilising, so use it with caution.

You should think long and hard about the actions you can take to improve and protect your cash flow position. For example, you could use a broker to help you get the best possible mortgage rate. You could also lock into a longer fixed-rate mortgage, as discussed above. There are lots of other actions you could take too.

Finally, the biggest thing you can do to improve your cash flow position is to buy the property at a lower price (or at least to resist overpaying for the property). In the next chapter, we're going to look at how to value residential property. We'll look at buying properties below market value (or BMV) and at a range of useful valuation tips and tricks used by the professionals to help you secure the best possible deal.

Chapter 3

How to value residential property

The preference, always, would be to buy a long-term franchise at a substantial discount from growing intrinsic value.

–Michael Burry, *Scion Capital*

In previous chapters, we've looked at rental yield calculations and we've learned all about the importance of cash flow. The next step in assessing a potential property deal is to work out how much a property is worth and to set a limit on the price that we're prepared to pay for it. To get to grips with that, we'll need to delve into the dark and murky world of property valuation. Are you strapped in? Hold tight. This could be a bumpy ride.

An introduction to property valuation

Property valuation is a professional discipline in itself. Valuations are commissioned by clients in a variety of different contexts, ranging from standard mortgage and land valuations to compulsory purchase orders and reinstatement costs for buildings insurance purposes.

Because of this wide variety of contexts, there are many ways to value property and a variety of techniques available to the professional valuer. The choice of method will be driven mainly by the purpose of the valuation. For example, a residential lease extension may warrant a different approach than a mortgage valuation. In addition, the availability (or not) of data may preclude the use of certain valuation techniques.

In this chapter, we're going to take a closer look at some commonly used property valuation terms and techniques. We'll introduce three methods for valuing residential properties that you can use straight out of the box. I'll also share some of my valuation tips and tricks, my special moves if you like, to help you pin down the price that you're prepared to pay for a property investment.

This chapter will focus exclusively on residential property, as that's my personal area of expertise. But if you'd like more information on valuing commercial property or developments, Property Valuation Principles by David Isaac is a great introduction. You can find details of this book in the references section.

Some important terminology

Like any other technical field, property valuation has its own lingo. Let's look at some of the commonly used terms. I've taken these definitions from the RICS Valuation Standards, but I've simplified them a little to make them a bit more accessible.

Market value

This is the estimated sale price of a property agreed between a willing buyer and a willing seller. It assumes the property is properly marketed and that each party has a good knowledge of the situation and acts without compulsion.

It's a straightforward definition, but it has lots of complexity built in. In particular, market value assumes the following: (a) market conditions at the valuation date will continue to apply at the date of the sale; (b) neither party is in an undue hurry to achieve a quick sale that could distort the price; (c) both parties are fully aware of the characteristics of the property.

You should keep this definition in mind when we discuss below market value (or BMV) property later.

Market rent

This is the estimated rental price of a property agreed between a willing lessor and a willing lessee. Again, it assumes the property is properly marketed and that each party has a good knowledge of the situation and acts without compulsion.

Market rent, therefore, is the rental equivalent of a property's market value. Because we're talking about rental value, we use the terms 'lessor and lessee' instead of 'buyer and seller'. Other than that, the working assumptions are similar to those used above.

Investment value

This is the value of a property to a particular owner or investor. Importantly, it's based on a working assumption about how the property will be used to generate income in the future.

Most property valuations use market reference points to estimate either the market value or the market rent. However, this type of valuation is based on the views of an individual purchaser and their anticipated use for a property. For example, an investor's valuation of a large house will probably differ depending on whether they intend to convert it into a professional HMO or operate it as a single-family buy-to-let. This is because their estimate of the potential income that can be generated will differ depending on the property's use.

The investment value can be similar to the market value, but it doesn't have to be. It builds in the investment return expectations of the investor and their view on the riskiness of the property. In short, this measure values a property at the price an investor needs to pay to meet their investment objectives.

So that's our key definitions and terminology sorted out. We now have a strong platform to build on for the rest of this chapter.

However, before we get into our three main valuation techniques, I'm going to digress for a moment to talk about one of the most misunderstood and potentially misleading terms in property.

An aside on below market value property

There's lots of talk in the property industry about buying below market value or BMV. This fascination with BMV deals appears to stem from the idea that buying below market value can help you grow your portfolio quicker by "baking in equity from day one". Personally, I blame Robert Kiyosaki of Rich Dad Poor Dad fame for all his talk about no-money down deals – eurgh.

But is buying below market value property even possible? Well, the short answer to this question is yes, absolutely. To see why, let's scan back to our definition of market value above. We can see that it's based on an idealised set of assumptions which may not hold in practice. For example: (a) the seller might be facing repossession and willing to accept a lower price for a quick sale; (b) the property may not have been marketed well, forcing the seller to reduce the price.

In this sense, buying below market value property is very much possible. However, it's not something that happens every day. After all, why would a seller accept less than the objective market value?

The trust but verify approach to BMV

Whilst buying BMV is theoretically possible, it's not easy to do. As such, you should retain a healthy scepticism for anyone marketing a property or an investment opportunity as BMV. If you do decide to consider these deals, you absolutely should factor their sourcing fee into your calculations and see if the deal still stacks up. The best approach is Ronald Reagan's – trust, but verify.

As a final word on this, it's important to acknowledge that market value itself is simply an estimate, not a fact. All valuations are opinions and they're based on assumptions. Typically, a professional valuation is expected to be within 10 per cent of the sale price achieved. However, the acceptable bracket can be bigger than 10 per cent in more challenging circumstances.

As such, anyone offering a discount of 10% BMV or less on a potential property deal is probably treading on thin ice. You know who you are. And by the way, don't send me any hate mail – it's bad for the environment and I'll just throw it in the recycling anyway.

Right, that's my rant on BMV over. With my integrity and my faith still intact, let's get on to our main topic.

Three ways to assess the value of a property

In this section, we're going to look at three ways to value residential property and how you can use them. Without further ado, let's introduce our first method.

1. The comparison method of valuation

Of our three methods, this is by far the most straightforward. As its name suggests, it relies on an analysis of previous transactions to give us an estimate of a property's market value. The idea is that if a similar property sold for a certain price, this tells us something about the market value.

The comparison method is simple and transparent. However, it does have its limitations. For example, some properties do not have direct comparables, perhaps because of their use, location, or other unique characteristics. Also, there may be no recent transactions.

How does the method work?

With this method, we analyse recent sold prices for similar transactions in the market. It tends to work best where there are regular transactions happening in the market and where there are properties similar in nature. As those ideal conditions deteriorate, so does the reliability of the comparison method.

The first step is to collect the raw data we need on comparables. These days, data is available from a range of sources, including the online portals like Rightmove and Zoopla and from HM Land Registry. The data you collect should be for similar properties that are close by and that have been sold recently.

Adjustments to the raw data

Once we've collected the raw data, we need to consider whether any adjustments are needed. For example, if one of our comparables has a floor space 10% bigger than the property we're trying to value, we should consider knocking 10% off the sold price of the comparable to account for this difference. Here's a list of some of the things we could consider adjusting for:

- *Usable space* – Any differences in the usable floor space.
- *Location factors* – If the house you're looking at is right next to a pub or a busy junction, the value will likely be lower than for an otherwise identical house in the same street.
- *Amenity* – The overall quality, desirability, or convenience of an area.
- *Aspect* – The specific positioning of a property, e.g. within a block, can have a significant effect on value. Ground floor flats tend to sell for less. Apartments with riverside views, double or triple aspects, and balconies, tend to sell for a higher price.
- *Rooms* – The number of bedrooms and bathrooms will affect the price, but we need to make sure we don't double count this versus the usable space.
- *Parking* – The presence or absence of onsite parking will also affect value.
- *Condition* – The condition of a property will affect its value too. Poorly maintained properties will be harder to sell, and buyers will discount properties by the sum needed to bring the condition in line with more marketable property.

Other factors could include the size of the garden, the standard of decor, the condition of the central heating system, the presence of double glazing, the condition of internal fixtures and fittings, and many other things that we haven't listed here.

How to use a sales schedule

We can keep track of all this data in a systematic manner on a *sales schedule*. A sales schedule brings together data for similar properties in one place. We can record the date the property was sold and the final sale price. We can also record the core characteristics of each of the properties, including the following: the number of bedrooms, bathrooms and parking spaces, any location factors, the aspect and the general condition. The sale schedule would show each property's usable floor space and from that a value per square-metre or per square-foot could be calculated.

A worked example

I've pulled together below a short example of how this works for an apartment block in Leeds. I know the block well because I own a two-bedroom apartment there myself. The table below shows the sold prices for the five most recent sales of two-bedroom apartments in the block. The price and date information are taken from HM Land Registry and the floor space data is taken from each property's EPC certificate, as these are also available free online.

Example sales schedule for five flats in a block in Leeds

Property	Sale price	Date sold	Floor space	No. of beds
Flat A	£273,500	03/09/19	76 m-sq	2
Flat B	£207,000	15/02/19	70 m-sq	2
Flat C	£250,000	19/12/18	76 m-sq	2
Flat D	£240,000	23/11/18	79 m-sq	2
Flat E	£255,000	04/01/18	71 m-sq	2

Because I know this block well, I know that most of the two-bedroom apartments also have two bathrooms, so I've ignored this here. Also, parking spaces are paid for separately when they are available.

Estimating a headline market value

Using this data, I can calculate an average price per square-metre of floor space. Across the five sales above, which go back roughly two years, the average price is around £3,300 per m-sq. If we look at just the last four properties, which are for sales over the last year, then the average is slightly lower at around £3,200 per m-sq. In determining the cut-off date to use in our average, there's a trade-off to be made. We want to use the most recent sales data, but we also need a sample size that's statistically credible. Here, I'm going to stick with the lower figure of £3,200 for the more recent sales data.

So, if we were trying to value my two-bedroom apartment, which has a floor space of 76 m-sq, our estimate of the market value could be in the range £240,000 to £250,000. We get this by multiplying the floor space of my apartment by the average price per square-metre, i.e. 76 m-sq × £3,200 per m-sq equals £243,200. I've put a bit of a range around the final estimate here to reflect the uncertainty involved in this process.

Any final adjustments

This estimate of the market value for my flat in Leeds feels about right based on my knowledge of this block in general. We could then adjust this value for any subjective factors, e.g. my flat is on a lower floor in the block and it's close to the train station platform, so you might reduce the price to account for this. Something in the range £230,000 to £240,000 feels about right given what I know about my apartment and how it compares with others in the block.

There's an element of subjectivity in any estimate. The better you know your local market, the better you'll be able to arrive at an estimate of the market value, including any adjustments needed.

Those who value properties for estate agents (and who are not always chartered surveyors) will tend to work on a more instinctive basis. They will have absorbed data on local market comparables through their interactions with the market over time. Essentially, they are doing a mental version of a sales schedule, making adjustments to their valuation as they go along based on the facts.

Final comments on the comparison method

Comparison lies at the heart of the property valuation process. In general, the comparison method works well for residential property. However, even in relatively straightforward cases, we need to adjust the market data to suit the specifics of the property we're trying to value. No two flats or houses are exactly the same, and we need to adjust the comparable data we use to suit the condition, location, and the characteristics of the property we're interested in.

There comes a point where the principle of comparing like-for-like becomes too stretched and where the comparison method breaks down. In these situations, we'll need to use some other valuation technique. However, comparison will still play a role in calibrating some of the other variables we'll use in our valuation. For example, we can also use the comparison method to estimate the market rent for a property, which can then be used as an input to some of the other valuation methods available to us.

As a final comment, I want to stress that you should never pay more than a property's market value. Ideally, you should be aiming to buy below its market value. Even though a certain property might be worth more to you than its objective market value (we'll come on to how you might decide this next) paying more than market value is a poor investment move. You may struggle to secure the financing you need or be forced to put more money down. You're also giving yourself no buffer against a potential future fall in property prices, which increases your risk in a potential forced sale scenario.

2. The investment method of valuation

The investment method of valuation is most useful for property investors. The method is a way to value a property from its actual or anticipated net rental income. It assumes an investor will look at the net rental yield and will be prepared to pay a multiple of that income to purchase the property. The investor's main reason for owning the property is not for occupation then, but for its financial reward from the flow of rental income and future potential for capital growth.

This method of property valuation is rooted in the individual investor's aims and objectives. As such, it's a much more subjective approach. It helps an investor to work out what they should pay for a property. And it's based on their goals and beliefs about a property's prospective future returns. If a property is well-located, in good condition and has a reliable tenant, it likely has good growth prospects. It will be highly sought after by investors who will be prepared to pay many times the net rental income to acquire the property. A property in poor condition in a secondary location leased to an unreliable tenant likely has poorer growth prospects. Investors will be willing to pay fewer multiples of the net rental income to acquire the property.

At the heart of this method is a determination of the net rental income an investor might expect from a property and the multiple that's used to 'capitalise' that rental income.

How does the method work?

The method begins with the relationship between the income from an investment and its purchase price or capital value. Where an investor has a minimum rate of return for a certain type of property, this can be factored into the mathematics.

The formula we will use to start the discussion is one we've already seen from Chapter One – that is, we'll start with the formula for the capitalisation rate of a property:

$$Cap \; rate = \frac{Net \; operating \; profit}{Purchase \; price}$$

We can rearrange this formula to give us the following:

$$Purchase \; price = \; Net \; operating \; profit/i$$

Here, i is the investor's required capitalisation rate from the property. Also, to recap, the net operating profit is the annual rental income less the annual rental costs, excluding mortgage costs. That's because cap rate assumes you purchase the property in full with no mortgage.

Let's look at a quick example of how this method works in practice.

A short worked example

Suppose you're interested in a one-bedroom apartment in Sheffield city centre. You've done your research and you've estimated the net operating profit to be £5,000 per year. If we require a capitalisation rate of 5% p.a. from an investment of this type, then we would be prepared to pay £5,000 p.a. ÷ 0.05 = £100,000 for this property.

In valuation parlance, this process *capitalises* the net operating profit of £5,000 p.a. to produce a capital value for the property. The multiple we used is 1 ÷ 0.05 = 20 times.

Finally, it's worth pointing out that the purchase price we've calculated is inclusive of all the potential purchase costs associated with the investment. That is, our £100,000 capital value includes all the stamp duty, legal fees, survey costs, mortgage broker fees, etc. So, we'd need to subtract these one-off costs off from our capital value to arrive at our offer price for the property.

How to set the capitalisation rate

In our previous chapter on cash flows, we talked in some detail about how to estimate net operating profit. So, we won't cover that again here. But how should an investor approach setting the capitalisation rate? After all, a small change in the cap rate used in the formula above changes the final purchase price significantly.

When setting the cap rate, an investor should take into account the trade-off between the risks posed by the investment and the potential for rental and capital growth. The 5% p.a. cap rate used in the example above suggests the investor is confident there will be some combination of rental and capital growth in the future. The investor may seek a higher cap rate on a property they consider riskier than this or a lower cap rate where the growth potential is even higher.

In Chapter One, we set out some rough indications around how capitalisation rates could vary with capital growth potential. Please note, however, that these types of rates move around over time as the economic backdrop changes. Let's take a closer look at this point.

Taking into account economic backdrop

When we're setting a cap rate for use in the investment method of valuation, we're deciding on the yield we'll accept for this property. However, that yield can and will move around based on the returns we can get on other types of investments. And I don't just mean property here, I mean the yield we can get on the full universe of potential investments, including stocks and shares, bonds, other types of property, etc.

One common reference point we can use is the current "risk-free" rate. In a UK context, this is often taken to be the yield you can get on long-term government bonds. It's based on the assumption that the UK government is unlikely to default on its debt. So, the yield on a long-term UK government bond sets a baseline for the return we could earn without taking any risk.

At the time of writing, the yield on a 20-year fixed interest UK government bond is hovering just below 1.0% p.a. – an all-time low. So, we could, for example, set our cap rate as a margin above this risk-free rate. The size of this margin, or risk premium as it's called, should increase with the perceived riskiness of the potential investment. In the past, investors have sought a risk premium of 3% to 6% p.a. over the risk-free rate on residential property, depending on the perceived riskiness of the investment. In the current environment, that would give a cap rate of somewhere between 4% and 7% p.a. for use in our calculations.

Taking into account borrowing costs

Another lens on this is the cost of borrowing. I'll use a quick example to help illustrate. Suppose I can borrow money at a cost of 3% p.a. If I borrow £100,000, the interest cost on my borrowing, assuming an interest only mortgage, would be £3,000 p.a. If I invest in a property which has a cap rate of 5% p.a., then I make £5,000 p.a. on the £100,000 of borrowed money invested. So, I'm okay to leverage here, as the cap rate is bigger than my borrowing cost. But suppose my cap rate is 3% p.a. In this case, I make £3,000 p.a. on the £100,000 of borrowed money I have invested, which is only just enough to cover my mortgage costs.

Based on the above, it only makes sense to leverage if my cap rate is bigger than my cost of borrowing. Flipping this on its head then, one way to set the cap rate is as a margin above the cost of borrowing for you as an investor. For example, if you can borrow long term at 3% p.a. on an interest-only mortgage, you might decide you'll accept a cap rate of between 1% and 4% p.a. over your 3% borrowing cost, depending on the rental and capital growth prospects for the property. Again, this would give us a cap rate of 4% to 7% p.a. But this time it's based on our own cost of borrowing.

Pulling it all together

The investment method is perhaps less intuitive to new investors than the comparison method. There's much more subjectivity involved, especially in the choice of capitalisation rate. But the method does have something good to offer. Firstly, it forces investors to decide on the yield they'll accept from an investment. Secondly, it forces a comparison with an investor's cost of borrowing and with the yields available on alternative investments. Lastly, it guides us on how we might flex our investment criteria with the economic backdrop.

In its simplest form as described above, the investment method can appear quite limited. For example, suppose I hold a view on how the rental profits of a property might change over time. Is it possible to build these beliefs into the valuation using the investment method? Well, the short answer is yes, but this requires us to extend the basic approach a little. So, before we wrap up our discussion of the investment method, we'll look at some common scenarios and how you can model these.

Under-rented property

An under-rented property is one which is let at a rental value lower than the current market rent. There is, therefore, an expectation that the rent will rise at the end of the tenancy. This situation is common in times of economic boom, where rents often lag the wider economy.

To take this into account in our valuation, the idea is that we'll use the market rent (sometimes call the estimated rental value or ERV by lettings agents) in our capitalisation calculation. But we'll also adjust for an amount of "lost rent" over the initial period until the current tenancy comes to an end.

Suppose in our example above the net operating profit of £5,000 p.a. is based on our best guess at the market rent of £650 pcm. However, the property was just let by the current landlord (the seller) on an 18-month tenancy at a below market rent of £600 pcm. In our valuation, we capitalise the £5,000 p.a. net operating profit, which is based on the market rent of £650 pcm, as £5,000 p.a. ÷ 0.05 = £100,000. We then subtract off the lost rent over the initial period until the tenancy can be reviewed and the rent can be increased. That is, we adjust the purchase price we're prepared to pay to £100,000 − 18 x (£650 − £600) = £99,100.

Over-rented property

An over-rented property is one which is let at a rental value higher than the current market rent. There is, therefore, an expectation that the rent will fall at the end of the tenancy. This situation is common for new build properties, where the first tenant might pay a small premium to live in a brand-new property. It's also common in an economic recession, where rents have fallen, but the existing tenancy was agreed before rents began to fall.

You can allow for an over-rented property in the opposite way to that used for an under-rented one. That is, use your estimate of the current market rent in your capitalisation calculation, then add on a premium to capture the extra rent currently being paid over and above the market rent.

The layer method

Under the layer method, we split our rental income into two parts. The first part is the current market rent, which is referred to as the *hardcore rent*. It is assumed to be a relatively certain core rent, and it's capitalised in the usual way. The second part is known as the *top slice*. The top slice is an uncertain additional income. It's capitalised using a higher cap rate (thereby putting a lower capital value on this extra slice of income) to reflect the uncertainty involved in achieving this additional income.

In volatile markets, there is some merit in separating the two elements of income this way. Let's look at an example. Suppose in our previous example that the net operating profit of £5,000 p.a. is based on a very certain hardcore rent of £650 pcm. We think we can rent this property out any day of the week for £650 pcm. However, we also think there's a good chance the property will rent for more than this in practice, say for £700 pcm, but we're not certain. In this case, we first capitalise the £5,000 p.a. based on the hardcore rent as £5,000 p.a. ÷ 0.05 = £100,000. We then capitalise the additional annual income of £600 p.a. (12 × £50 pcm of extra rent) as £600 p.a. ÷ 0.07 ≈ £8,600. This gives us a purchase price of £100,000 + £8,600 = £108,600 for this property.

Note that we used a higher cap rate of 7% p.a. to capitalise the top slice of rent to reflect the higher risk and greater uncertainty of achieving this particular slice of additional income.

The layer method can also be used in situations where the top slice is expected to materialise later, say in five or ten years. For a more detailed discussion on the layer method please see Property Valuation Principles by David Isaac.

Modelling a light refurb

Finally, let's consider the case of a light refurbishment. Suppose you've spotted a gem of a property somewhere in the Northern Powerhouse. It needs a bit of work to capture its maximum rental price, say it needs some new carpets and a lick of paint. However, we expect the refurb to be a light one, so we can be relatively certain about the cost of the overall works.

In this situation, I would use a net rental income based on the market rent after the work had been carried out in my capitalisation calculation. I'd look at similar properties and what they're currently renting for, but I'd pick comparables based on what I expect the property to look like after the works have been completed. Then, I would subtract off my estimate of the cost of doing the works from the purchase price I'm prepared to pay.

Because this project is straightforward, I wouldn't build in a buffer for things going wrong. In addition, these light refurbishment projects tend to be quite keenly priced in the market, so I wouldn't build in a profit margin for my efforts, unless I was planning to sell the property. For larger projects, however, this is exactly the kind of thinking you should be doing. That brings us to our third and final valuation method.

3. The residual method of valuation

Our final method is the residual method of valuation. Property developers use this method to estimate the price they're prepared to pay for a piece of land that they intend to develop. To do this, they estimate the final value of a completed development and subtract off the cost of the development and their profit margin to arrive at a *residual land value*. That is, they use the method to work out what they're prepared to pay for the land itself.

The average buy-to-let property investor is unlikely to be taking on large-scale development projects. However, we can use this approach to work out the price we're prepared to pay for a property that needs a large amount of work doing before we can let it out or perhaps sell. That is, we can use the method to estimate how much we should pay for a property that we're intending to refurbish. Let's take a closer look at this.

How does the method work?

The basic process for the residual method of valuation works as follows.

1.   Value of the property at completion

- If we're buying to sell, we should use the comparison method to estimate the final sale price of the property after all the works have been completed.
- If we're buying to let, we can use the investment method to work out what the property is worth to us as a buy-to-let investment based on net profit.

2.   Less the cost of carrying out the development

- Costs should include all the materials, labour and project management fees
- It should include any financing costs, e.g. loan interest, arrangement fees, etc incurred in the development period
- We also need to build in a profit margin as our reward for doing the development in the first place
- It should include all ancillary purchase costs, e.g. stamp duty, legal fees, broker and valuation fees, etc
- If we're buying to sell, there will also be selling costs

3.   Equals the amount we should pay for the property

So, the method sounds straightforward, but there's lots that could go wrong at each stage of the estimation process. As such, this method is prone to error, and it can give a wide range of answers, depending on the various assumptions and cost estimates made.

Estimating the cost of a refurbishment

To estimate the cost of a refurbishment, you could ask for quotes from a builder. You can also speak to local agents about the potential cost of the works.

If you're looking to get a rough feel for the likely cost to see if the project is even viable to begin with, you can estimate these yourself using a *schedule of works*. For example, you could use a simple spreadsheet, something like the following, to estimate the cost.

Example schedule of works for a refurbishment project

Item	Price	Quantity	Cost
Redecoration			
Stripping (per room)	£200	3	£600
Plastering (per room)	£250	3	£750
Painting (per room)	£150	3	£450
Cost of redecoration			£1,800
Windows and doors			
Double glazing (per window)	£500	0	£0
Internal door (per door)	£100	3	£300
Internal fire door (per door)	£150	1	£150
External fire door (per door)	£550	1	£550
Cost of window and doors			£1,000
etc			

In this way, you can estimate the cost of the refurbishment using a bottom-up approach and then verify this figure with a local builder. Other costs to think about include replacing the central heating and boiler systems, electrical works, new floorings, perhaps the cost of a new kitchen or bathroom, if needed, any costs associated with the roofing and exterior of the building, etc.

You should build in a contingency to allow for potential errors in your estimation too. For example, you could include a contingency of 10% of the total estimated cost to guard against overruns.

Other associated costs

If you're using bridging finance, you should build this cost into your calculations. Be prudent in your estimate of how many weeks or months it will take to complete the development, as you don't want to underestimate the financing costs involved.

You will also want to include a profit margin as your reward for the time, energy and capital cost of undertaking the project. Developers use different approaches here. The approach I like to use is to calculate the profit as a % of the cash tied up in the project. For example, say the cash you need to complete the development is £100,000. This includes the deposit amount, stamp duty and other purchase costs, the development and financing costs, etc. Then I might require a profit of 20% of £100,000 which is £20,000 as my reward for undertaking this project.

Final comments on the residual method

The outcome of the residual valuation can be susceptible to changes in the variables involved, including development costs, financing costs, delays and project overruns, etc. The method is, however, often the only realistic way of getting to a valuation figure where some sort of large-scale property development work is involved.

If you're going to use this method in flips or refurbishments, then make sure that you're putting in enough of a contingency to avoid a loss. Also, do make sure you get input from experienced property developers, builders, and local agents to increase the accuracy of your calculations. This is likely to be particularly important in your first few developments or if you're taking on a project beyond your comfort zone. Use other people's experience to supplement your own to help you get a better outcome.

You can also use sensitivity analysis to show how your profit might change as the key variables in your residual valuation change. For example, if you're doing a flip, you could run the numbers assuming a +/- 10 per cent change in the development cost and +/- 5% in the final sale price.

In conclusion

That brings us to the end of this chapter on property valuation techniques. Hopefully you now feel much wiser and more equipped to deal with any property valuation tasks ahead of you.

We've just scratched the surface of a vast topic here. There are plenty of good books out there on property valuation. So, if you're interested, you should check some of these out. You'll be able to read all about more advanced valuation techniques like discounted cash flow modelling, how commercial property differs from residential property, and how to build the impact of inflation explicitly into your valuation and modelling.

Which of these techniques is most useful to you will really depend on your property strategy. If you're interested in plain, simple buy-to-lets, the investment method will likely be of most interest to you. If you trade properties for a living, then you'll likely be most interested in the comparison method and buying below market value property. If you're flipping, then you'll be making use of the residual method of valuation combined with the comparison method to estimate the final sale price for the property.

Finally, as a follow-up to my earlier rant on below market value deals, please do beware of scammers and rip-off merchants touting BMV property deals. It's okay to look at these deals, but please make sure you do your own due diligence to see if the deal stacks up and if their claims make sense. Remember, if a deal sounds too good to be true, then it probably is.

Chapter 4

Calculations for deal financing

Give me a lever long enough and a fulcrum on which to place it, and I shall move the world.

–Archimedes

Financing your property portfolio is just as important as finding great deals to invest in. Without the right finance, your property portfolio will take a longer to grow. What's more, you'll miss out on one of the most powerful tools in the investor's toolkit – leverage.

In this chapter, we'll take a closer look at leverage and how you can use it to enhance your returns. We'll also look at different types of mortgage, the mortgage stress testing rules for buy-to-let property investors in the UK, and at some of the hidden costs of investing through a limited company.

This chapter has the potential to supercharge your investment journey. Financing a property portfolio correctly using leverage is like injecting nitro into its engine. Fast and furious it certainly is not, but over the long-term it has the power to greatly enhance returns.

What is leverage?

Leverage is one of those words property investors throw around all the time. But what does it mean? Here we're talking specifically about financial leverage. And by financial leverage, we simply mean using borrowed money to invest in assets. That is, when we buy a property, we put in some of the money ourselves and we use money borrowed from a lender or a bank to purchase the rest.

If you told your non-investor friend about this idea over coffee, their likely reaction would be "isn't that really risky?" or something similar. The short answer to this question is yes. Leverage increases your risk, as taking on debt is always destabilising. So, financing your portfolio using loans and mortgages does increase its riskiness. But if you borrow carefully and sensibly, leverage also has the potential to boost your returns dramatically.

We'll look at the two ways borrowing can add juice to your returns shortly. But firstly, let's look at some mortgage basics.

The two main types of mortgage

The two main types of mortgage you can use to invest in buy-to-let properties are repayment and interest only mortgages.

Repayment mortgage

With a repayment mortgage, you pay off a small amount of the loan each month plus interest. By the end of the term, you will have paid off the loan in full. Because you pay off the loan gradually, your monthly payments will be higher than an interest only mortgage.

Interest only mortgage

With an interest only mortgage, you pay just the interest on the borrowed money each month. At the end of the mortgage term, you still need to pay back the original amount borrowed. So, you'll need a plan for how to pay this back at the end of the term.

Most owner-occupiers take out repayment mortgages. Their thinking is that they want to have the mortgage paid off in full by the time they retire. So, they opt to pay this off gradually over time. This is the default for most property owners and it's favoured by banks.

Property investors, however, typically opt for interest only mortgages. Their thinking is that it requires lower monthly payments, so it improves the investor's cash flow position. The investor then has the choice of whether to use the extra cash flow to overpay on the mortgage, thereby reducing their outstanding mortgage balance, or put it towards their next property purchase instead.

If you're not overly comfortable with the general idea of debt, then a repayment mortgage might appear to be a safer choice. However, it's really a matter of personal preference. And if your plan is to grow a large property portfolio, you'll likely want to opt for an interest only mortgage and reinvest that extra cash flow.

How to estimate your mortgage payments

Let's take a quick look at how to estimate the payments you'll need to make for each of these mortgage types.

Payments on an interest only mortgage

If your interest only mortgage has a 3% p.a. interest rate, it means that every year you will need to pay the lender 3% of the total loan amount. For example, if you take out a loan of £100,000, the interest will be £100,000 × 3% which equals £3,000 each year. To calculate the monthly payments, simply divide this amount by 12 – that is, £3,000 ÷ 12 = £250 per month.

Time for a quick formula. If the loan amount is A and our interest rate is i, then we have the following formulae for our payments:

$$Annual\ payment = A \times i$$

and

$$Monthly\ payment = (A \times i)/12$$

I typically use the monthly formulae, as I tend to model cash flows on a monthly basis. But you can use whichever formulae works for you.

Payments on a repayment mortgage

To estimate the payments due on a repayment mortgage, we need a slightly more complicated calculation. Here we have A as the loan amount, i as the interest rate and T as the term of the mortgage. We then have the following formulae for our payments:

$$Annual\ payment = \frac{A \times i}{(1 - (1+i)^{-T})}$$

and

$$Monthly\ payment = \frac{1}{12} \times \left(\frac{A \times i}{(1 - (1+i)^{-T})} \right)$$

Let's work through a quick example. Suppose we take out a loan of £100,000 for a term of 25 years at an interest rate of 3% p.a. Our annual payment amount will be calculated as follows:

$$\frac{£100,000 \times 0.03}{(1 - 1.03^{-25})} = £5,743$$

Our monthly payments will then be around £5,743 ÷ 12 = £479. This is around double the monthly payment due on an interest only mortgage of £250 per month which we calculated above using the same loan amount and the same rate of interest.

I won't go into the derivation of the formula here, but rest assured it's a tried and tested one. There are a couple of things you should know about it though. Firstly, it assumes your mortgage payments are made annually in arrears – that is, all at once at the end of the year. In practice, you'll likely need to make payments on a monthly basis throughout the year, so the payments required will actually be slightly less than the estimate provided by this formula.

The cheat's formula for repayment mortgages

If the above formula is too much of a hassle or if you don't have a scientific calculator to hand, then you can use my cheat's formula for repayment mortgages instead. It only gives a rough answer, but it's useful as a calculation you can do in your head without a scientific calculator or a spreadsheet tool to hand:

$$Annual\ payment = \frac{A}{T} + \frac{A \times i}{2}$$

and

$$Monthly\ payment = \frac{1}{12} \times \left(\frac{A}{T} + \frac{A \times i}{2} \right)$$

Let's run through a quick example again. Using the same scenario as above, we have a loan of £100,000 with a term of 25 years at an interest rate of 3% p.a. Our annual payment amount due will be calculated as follows:

$$\frac{£100,000}{25} + \frac{£100,000 \times 0.03}{2} = £5,500$$

Our monthly payments will then be around £5,500 ÷ 12 = £458. This is close to the £479 per month figure that we get using the more accurate formula above and it's generally a good estimate.

A short aside for the maths geeks

To see why the cheat's formula works, we can break it down into parts. With a repayment mortgage, we're spreading the repayments for the loan of amount A over T years. So, the A ÷ T bit of the formula gives us the amount needed per year to repay the loan by the end of the term. To estimate the average interest paid per year is a bit more complicated. In our cheat's formula, we simply say that at the start of the term we owe the full amount A back to the bank, so our annual interest cost will be A × i, but by the end of the term we owe the bank nothing, so our annual interest cost will be nil. As such, the average interest paid in any one year is the average of A × i and nil which equals (A × i) ÷ 2. Our estimate of the annual mortgage cost is then the sum of these two parts, giving us the cheat's formula above.

Wrapping this up

Right, that's quite enough geekery around mortgage calculations for one day. I hope that's useful to you as an introduction to the topic. If you do need a mortgage calculator, there's a couple of nice ones available free online. Simply do a search for these online.

For the rest of this chapter, I'm going to assume that you will use an interest only mortgage when you're financing your property portfolio, as that's what most investors do in practice. You can adjust the calculations yourself if you plan to use a repayment mortgage.

Using leverage to enhance your returns

Using leverage can help to enhance the returns generated on your property portfolio. There are two aspects to this.

Harnessing the power of capital growth

Suppose you have £100,000 to invest. Should you use the £100,000 to buy one property outright with no borrowing or should you buy four properties, each worth £100,000, using a mortgage of £75,000 and a deposit of £25,000 on each? Well, let's look at what could happen to the value of your portfolio in each case.

Let's say that over the next five years property prices increase by 10%. In the first case, your portfolio will have increased in value by £10,000. The return generated from capital growth over this period is 10%. That is, £10,000 divided by the £100,000 invested.

In the second case, the value of your portfolio will have increased by £40,000 – from £400,000 to £440,000. That is, you'll have made £10,000 on each of the four properties you bought. And the return generated from capital growth is now 40%. That is, it's £40,000 divided by the £100,000 you invested.

This example illustrates how you can use leverage to increase your returns. I've ignored some of the detail here, e.g. like transaction fees, buying and selling expenses, etc. But you get the idea.

So, what's the catch? Well, leverage can work against you when prices fall. Suppose property prices had fallen by 10%, rather than increased. In the first case above, you would have lost only 10% of your investment, but in the second case you'd have lost 40% of your initial investment. This is only an issue if you are forced to sell in a falling market and crystallise these losses. But if you can hold on until the market recovers then you're fine. The key to riding out a dip in the market is to make sure you're cash flow positive, which we've covered at length in Chapter Two.

Adding some juice to your ROI

As well as harnessing the power of capital growth, leverage can also increase your ROI. To see how this works, we're going to derive a new formula. Firstly, let's define a few terms:

r_c = capitalisation rate
r_b = borrowing rate
P = purchase price
D = deposit % (i.e. % of purchase price we've put down)
$(1 - D)$ = loan-to-value (i.e. % of purchase price borrowed)

Consider the case where we buy one property outright with no borrowing. The return on our cash is simply the capitalisation rate for the property, or r_c. That is, because we've put down 100% of the money to buy the property ourselves, our ROI is equal to r_c.

But what if we put down only a certain percentage of the purchase price and borrow the rest of the money. We can derive a simple formula to calculate our ROI based on the variables above.

$$ROI = \frac{[r_c \times P - r_b \times (1 - D) \times P]}{D \times P}$$

On the top of the fraction we have our annual net operating profit as $r_c \times P$, which gives us the net income from the unlevered property, less our cost of borrowing as $r_b \times (1 - D) \times P$. This then is the annual rental profit from our property after the borrowing costs are taken into account. Finally, we divide through by the cash invested, i.e. $D \times P$, to get our return on investment or ROI.

Let's simplify this formula a little with some mathematics:

$$ROI = \frac{r_c \times P}{D \times P} - \frac{r_b \times (1 - D) \times P}{D \times P}$$

$$= \frac{r_c}{D} - \frac{r_b \times (1 - D)}{D}$$

$$= \frac{r_c}{D} - \frac{r_b}{D} + r_b$$

which gets us to

$$ROI = r_b + (r_c - r_b)/D$$

Using our new formula

The derivation of the formula is not important, so don't worry too much if you didn't follow the mathematics here. What is important is understanding the final result. So now that we've got the final formula we need, let's take a look at how leverage can enhance your ROI.

Suppose that $r_c > r_b$, that is, our cap rate is bigger than our cost of borrowing. Then the term on the right of the above equation is positive, i.e. $(r_c - r_b)$ is positive. As our D gets smaller, that is we put down a smaller deposit amount, then $(r_c - r_b)/D$ gets bigger (we're dividing through by a smaller number). As such, when our deposit amount decreases, our ROI increases.

This is how leverage works to enhance your overall ROI.

Let's take a look at a quick numerical example. Suppose that our borrowing cost $r_b = 3\%$ p.a. and that the capitalisation rate for the property $r_c = 4.5\%$ p.a. Then ROI varies with the deposit amount D as set out in the following table.

How our ROI varies with the deposit percentage

D	ROI
100%	4.5%
75%	5.0%
50%	6.0%
25%	9.0%

We can see from this table that in the case where we buy the property outright, i.e. $D = 100\%$, then our ROI is equal to our cap rate. As our deposit percentage decreases from 100% to 25%, our ROI increases from 4.5% p.a. to 9.0% p.a. That's the power of leverage.

Finding the sweet spot

So, leverage can be used to power up our ROI. But it's worth pointing out that as our deposit amount decreases, our monthly cash flow from the investment will decrease because of the higher borrowing costs. In practice, therefore, the amount of leverage you're comfortable with will depend on how much of a cash flow buffer you want from your investment. Ultimately, it's a trade-off you need to make – a lower deposit amount gives a better ROI, but a higher one will give a better margin for safety on your cash flow. You'll need to find the sweet spot in the middle that you're happy with.

As a final word of caution, leverage will only increase your ROI if your cap rate is bigger than your cost of borrowing. You can see from the formula above that if $r_c < r_b$, then the term on the right, that is $(r_c - r_b)$, will be negative. In this case, the lower the deposit amount, the more negative the term on the right becomes and hence the lower your ROI. So when $r_c < r_b$, using more leverage will only make things worse from an ROI perspective. That's why a sensible way to set the cap rate you require from an investment is as a margin over your cost of borrowing, as we discussed in the last chapter.

The long-term impact of inflation

As we noted earlier, property prices over much of the 20th century tracked around inflation plus 0.5% p.a. in both the US and the UK. As such, over the long-term, it would be a reasonable assumption that this would continue to be the case, albeit that price growth is unlikely to be in a straight line.

We've seen from the above that if property prices increase, then using leverage has the power to harness that capital growth to produce outsized returns. The fact that property prices tend to rise with inflation over the long term means we're highly likely to benefit from using leverage to build our portfolio.

It's worth pointing out that inflation will have an impact on our ROI over time too. Rents in the UK tend to rise in line with wage inflation. Over the long-term, average salaries have risen in line with inflation plus around 0.5% to 1.0% p.a. depending on the historical period you look at. As such, we can expect our top line rental income to increase with inflation over the long-term.

Repayments on our mortgage will be fixed, and this is likely to be our biggest expense. However, other expenses like ground rents, service charges, management fees, etc will likely increase in line with inflation too. In addition, as our property ages, we're likely to spend more on upkeep and maintenance. Over time, the combined effect of all these factors means the profitability of our investment and our ROI will likely increase, but to a smaller extent than might be expected from the headline growth in rental income.

Over the long-term, the impact of inflation combined with leverage has the power to boost the returns you experience from both capital growth and day-to-day rental profits.

How much can you borrow?

So, we've looked at the power of leverage to enhance your investment returns. The next thing to discuss is how much you can borrow and whether the banks will lend to you at all.

When it comes to buy-to-let, the amount you can borrow is less about the creditworthiness of you as a borrower and more about the investment proposition itself. Lenders will be interested in the market value of the property. Ultimately, this is what the property is worth to them if you default on your mortgage payments and they need to sell the property to recoup the loan. Lenders will also be interested in the rental income the property generates, as they want the investment to be self-financing, i.e. capable of meeting the repayments by itself.

Tests that the lenders apply

Let's take a quick look at some of the tests that lenders will apply when determining how much you can borrow for a buy-to-let.

Loan-to-value

In general, the maximum loan-to-value or LTV on a buy-to-let property investment is around 85%. The most typical level is 75%. So, if you want to buy a property for £100,000, the minimum deposit amount might be £15,000, but you'll more likely need a deposit of £25,000 or greater.

You can, of course, always borrow lower amounts. At 60% loan-to-value, mortgage interest rates typically start to decrease. So, this might be something to consider if you want to improve your cash flow and if you're prepared to put down a larger deposit.

In addition, please note that lending criteria do change over time, so you should check with a mortgage broker in advance of looking for your next deal, rather than relying on these rules of thumb.

Rental cover

Lenders use a second criteria called rental cover to assess whether the investment is self-financing.

Most lenders insist that the rental income must be at least 125% of the mortgage payment, but assessed using a higher interest rate of at least 5.5% p.a. This ratio of the rental income to the monthly mortgage payments is known as the *interest coverage ratio* or ICR.

Let's look at an example

Say that your interest only mortgage payments are £250 per month at an interest rate of 3.0% p.a. The lender will calculate what the payments would be at the higher interest rate of 5.5% p.a. That is, the mortgage payments would be £250 ×

5.5% / 3.0% or £458 per month. They then multiply this by 125% to get £573 per month. So, the lender will only lend if they believe the market rent on the property will be £573 per month or higher.

For an interest only mortgage, we can use the following formula to calculate the minimum rental income required per month. The ICR is the interest coverage ratio specified by the lender and i is the interest rate used to calculate the actual monthly mortgage payment.

$$Rent\ required\ =\ ICR \times \frac{5.5\%}{i} \times Actual\ mortgage\ (per\ month)$$

Different lenders have different criteria. The PRA lending regulations require at least 125% rental cover, but some lenders will use a higher ICR percentage, e.g. 135% or 145%.

Finally, it's worth saying that these criteria don't apply to lending on more specialist property investments like commercial property, HMOs, and holiday lets. They also don't apply to lending with a fixed term of five years or more.

Before you weigh up a deal, make sure you've lined up a good mortgage broker. That way, you can get the latest updates from them on the different lenders before you start to model a deal.

What will the lender want to know about you?

Although the lenders' focus will be on the profitability and security of the proposed investment, they will also want to vet the person they're lending too. Typical things lenders look at include the following:

- your non-property income
- whether you own your own home
- previous property experience
- where you live, e.g. in the UK or abroad
- whether you're buying through a limited company

There are thousands of products available for buy-to-let investors. Some of these might be ruled out, depending on your circumstances and your level of experience.

However, a good broker should be able to help you get the best product for you, factoring in your personal circumstances and any restrictions.

A few thoughts on mortgage products

When it comes to the mortgage product, there are lots of different variables in play. Your mortgage broker will be able to help you pick out the best deal from those on offer. However, it also helps to know your own preferences on these parameters too. So, here are a few thoughts on the different variables that you'll need to pin down.

Loan-to-value

Most investors choose something at the higher end of the range, say a 75% LTV. However, there's nothing to stop you going for a 60% or lower LTV if you want to use less leverage, secure a better interest rate and improve that monthly cash flow position.

Fixed or variable interest rates

The interest rate can be fixed or variable. Common fixed rate products will fix the interest rate for say two, five or ten years. Afterwards, they typically revert to a variable rate set as a margin above the base rate set by the Bank of England or perhaps LIBOR.

Variable rate products might have an interest rate set to the lender's standard variable rate. Lenders can change this at their will. Again, it could be set as a margin above the base rate or LIBOR.

In general, I tend to go for longer fixed rate mortgage products, e.g. with a fixed rate of five years or more. Interest costs are usually a property investor's biggest expense. So, for me, it makes sense to take the risk out of this by fixing the cost for a longer period. Also, there are a bunch of hidden costs involved in re-mortgaging, e.g. legal expenses, valuation costs and product fees. This means I want to re-mortgage as few times as possible. Not to mention that re-mortgaging can be a total time-drag and it's often not as easy to get the refinancing over the line as it looks on paper.

Independent Legal Advice

I also have a final word of warning on re-mortgages for those buying through a limited company. Lenders will often require Directors of the limited company to sign a personal guarantee for the loan and will ask them to take Independent Legal Advice (ILA) on this matter. This is a bit of a grey area and one that can add to the cost of a re-mortgage. This legal advice can sometimes cost £250 to £300 per director or more. Certain lenders might be willing to waive the ILA requirement, or they may be happy for this to be provided by the conveyancing solicitor, which can reduce the cost slightly. If you're in this position, you should speak to your mortgage broker to see what the best options are here.

Product fees

Certain of the products will also come with an arrangement fee. This can be a fixed amount (e.g. like £995) or set as a percentage of the total amount borrowed (e.g. 0.5% or 1.0%). You will often have the option of having them add this fee to the loan amount. I tend to take this option, as it means that you don't have to pay out the cash right away, so it improves your cash flow.

In conclusion

In this chapter, we've covered the nuts and bolts of using mortgages to finance your property portfolio. We've explored the concept of leverage and how it can help to boost your returns, both the returns from capital growth and your day-to-day rental returns. In this way, using leverage does increase the heat – it's like adding some cayenne pepper to your chilli bean stew. Is that enough of the cheesy analogies for now? Maybe just one more.

However, with great power comes great responsibility. Leverage can work against you in a falling property market, making it even more important that your portfolio remains cash flow positive and that you're never a forced seller at the bottom of the market. The best defence here is a good offence. That is, you should use cash flow modelling and stress testing to make sure you understand the risks involved and only go for those deals where you have a good margin for safety.

We also proved, using a nifty bit of mathematics, that your cap rate needs to be bigger than your cost of borrowing. Otherwise, using leverage will only worsen your ROI.

Nassim Taleb's bar bell strategy

As a final word on debt in general, many new investors are rightly concerned about taking on large amounts of debt. For some people, this could be a mental blocker that prevents them from financing a property portfolio using debt or even from getting into property in the first place. If you fall into this category, then there are strategies you can employ which might help here.

In his excellent and thought-provoking book Antifragile, Nassim Taleb talks about his now famous bar bell strategy for harnessing the power of uncertainty to your advantage. The idea here is to put your portfolio in a position where you are indifferent to property prices rising or falling, since you can't predict in advance which direction they will go in. If you're buying property using leverage, then you'll do well in a rising market, but you run the risk of being wiped out in a falling market. To combat this, you could, for example, always keep a large chunk of cash in the bank. So, when the market crashes, you can use this cash buffer to ride out the market dip. You can also use it as a tactical fund to buy additional properties at knocked-down prices with great yields.

Your leveraged property investments sit at one side of the bar bell and mean you'll do well in a rising market. Your opportunistic cash fund is the counterweight that sits at the other side of the bar bell. It's the bit that will help you make the most of the opportunities available in a falling market.

Chapter 5

Ten negotiation tips and tricks

When the final result is expected to be a compromise, it is often prudent to start from an extreme position.

–John Maynard Keynes
The Economic Consequences of the Peace

Our final chapter in Part One is all about property negotiations. I'll present a range of tips and tricks that you can use to strike better property deals. You'll also be able to use them in other walks of life too, like getting the kids to go to bed on time – a bonus for all you time-strapped parents out there.

Many of the techniques and strategies discussed in this chapter are based on Chris Voss's thought-provoking book Never Split the Difference. Chris is a former FBI hostage negotiator. He honed his craft in the high-stakes world of hostage negotiations. And what's good enough to help Chris save lives is good enough for us. I've adapted a number of the techniques discussed in the book, and I'll show you how to use them in property negotiations. There's also a cheeky bonus tip at the end too, so keep reading to make sure you get that one.

Why property negotiations are different

In a typical property negotiation, there is little direct contact (if any) between the buyer and seller. Most of the time, you'll be negotiating through a third-party, such as an estate agent or a broker. That means your ability to directly assess the wants and needs of the counterparty will usually be limited. This single fact makes property negotiations different from most other types of negotiation. It's also why certain negotiation techniques will work (and others won't) and why you'll have to do things a bit differently to get a great outcome.

I'm sure you're excited to get started and so am I. So, let's look at our first negotiation tip.

My top ten negotiation tips and tricks

Here are my top ten negotiation tips and tricks. They're presented roughly in the order you might want to use them in a typical property negotiation. However, a few of the later ones are general concepts that you can use at any point in the deal lifecycle.

Negotiation Tip # 1 – Proof of Life

There is a technique in hostage negotiation called *proof of life*. You'll be familiar with this concept already from Hollywood blockbusters. The idea is that the negotiator (our hero) will refuse to enter the negotiation unless the hostage taker provides proof of life. This could be putting the hostage on the telephone or sending one of those classic photos of the hostage holding up a copy of today's newspaper. It's the way the kidnapper proves he's got the thing we're after.

But how can you use this technique in property negotiations I hear you ask? Well, in business deals, we can use the technique as a kind of "proof of life of the deal". That is, we can ask a question or create a hoop that someone needs to jump through to earn the right to do business with us. The test we use is designed to open the dialogue in a professional way and their answer will indicate whether they plan on doing business with us and whether they can be trusted to honour their subsequent agreements.

What kinds of things can we ask for?

In the past, I've used a variety of questions to open proceedings. I usually try to ask for some additional piece of information that helps me with my modelling. For example, you could ask for things like:

- details of the current service charge and ground rent
- a copy of the tenancy agreement (if the property is tenanted)
- a copy of the lease agreement to check things like ground rent increases and/or your ability to sublet
- any fees that will be applied by the freeholder on subletting the property
- your rights around changes or repairs to the property

You can ask for anything you think will be helpful to you. Ideally, the request will need a little bit (but not a lot) of effort to dig out. The request should be presented to the estate agent as something that you need before you can put an offer in on the property. In effect, therefore, the seller's reward for this little bit of effort is that they get to hear your offer.

The response you get and the time they take to get back to you will tell you something about the seller and give you a feeling for how keen they are to do a deal. If used correctly, the technique is also a way of demonstrating your credibility and that you know what you're talking about. That brings us nicely on to tip number two.

Negotiation Tip # 2 – Establish your credibility

For our offer to be taken seriously, we need to establish ourselves as a credible counterparty. In Robert Cialdini's famous book Influence, authority is one of the six factors he discusses that can increase your ability to influence others. That is, people are more likely to listen to and act on requests from authority figures like policemen, doctors, judges, etc. And within their domain of expertise, these professionals receive a sort of automatic credibility that they can leverage to their advantage.

Let's be clear. I'm not for a second suggesting you should pretend to be a doctor when buying your next property. (It might not be a bad idea in practice though.)

What I am suggesting is that you should do everything you can to establish yourself as a credible and reliable person to do business with. This is most important when you're dealing with someone new and who you have no existing track record with. You'll want to come across as professional, experienced and preferably likeable too.

How can we do this in practice?

When you're dealing with a new agent or seller, you can tell them a little bit about yourself and your background to establish your credibility. This could include telling them about things like:

- your experience as a property investor
- what you do for a day-job / your occupation
- where you are in your property journey
- any past experiences investing in their local area
- details of any relevant deals you've done

If you've got a good team around you, e.g. an accountant, mortgage broker, solicitor, then you can leverage this too. For example, by saying you'll need to run a point past your broker, you'll present yourself as an established investor with a strong team.

If you've got good relationships with a mutual contact, e.g. another agent in the same city, you might be able to leverage that relationship to establish some credibility. A word of warning though that this technique can backfire if your relationship with the mutual contact is not as strong as you think.

And finally, make sure the agent knows you have your financing fully lined up or that you have a plan to arrange this quickly. It boosts the credibility of your offer if you have financing lined up in advance. You should also provide proof of funds if you can.

Optional extra: The Chris Discount

In Never Split the Difference, Voss talks about how simply using your own name can help you in negotiations.

In a hostage negotiation, using a hostage's name in front of the kidnapper and getting the kidnapper to use it back can help humanise the hostage. This in turn makes it less likely that the hostage will be harmed. In the same way, using your own name creates the dynamic of "forced empathy". That is, it forces the counterparty to see you as a real person.

Chris tells a great story of how he asked a store in an outlet mall for a discount using the line 'My name is Chris. What's the Chris discount?'. The answer, incidentally was 10%. In short, therefore, humanise yourself. Use your name to introduce yourself. Be fun, be friendly. And get your own special discount.

Negotiation Tip # 3 – No kicks off the negotiation

Getting a "Yes" is the final goal of every negotiation. But you shouldn't aim for it right away. Saying "No" makes people feel safe, secure, and in control. So, you should aim to trigger a "No" early in the process. By rejecting your offer, your counterpart will start to define the space for negotiation in their own minds. They will also gain the confidence and comfort to listen to your next offer properly.

Early on in my own investment journey, I was super keen to do a deal. I'd read the books, done my research, and saved up that first deposit. The only thing standing in my way was the other party saying "Yes" to my offer. But my over-eagerness prevented me from being an effective negotiator. I got disheartened when my first offer was rejected and quickly upped my offer, only to get a second rejection. I did finally get to a "Yes", but the price was way more than I wanted to pay. In short, I negotiated against myself to the point where a deal was no longer possible.

Great negotiators seek a "No" early on because that's when the real negotiation begins. Before you get to a deal, the other party will need to convince themselves that the solution you wanted works for them or even better that it was their own idea. They'll only get to this place by going through "No" first. You won't beat them with logic or brute force. Remember that to get to a deal – it's not about you, it's about them.

Negotiation Tip # 4 – Use an extreme anchor

Going first is not necessarily best when it comes to negotiating price. For example, you might offer more than the seller was expecting to receive and end up paying more than you needed. But when you think about it, this is exactly the set-up for most property negotiations. That is, the buyer puts in an offer which the seller then considers.

So how can we protect our interests here? Voss suggests using a psychological technique known as the anchor and adjustment effect. Researchers have discovered that we tend to make adjustments from our first reference point. That's because we focus on the initial number and then extrapolate. And we end up depending too heavily on the initial piece of information offered (the "anchor") when making later decisions.

Let's talk through a quick example. Suppose there's a lovely one-bedroom apartment in Leeds that's on the market for £115,000. The top price you're prepared to pay is £102,500 from your modelling, which is a lot lower than the seller's asking price. To get a price movement of this order, you will need to go for an extreme low anchor that squishes their hopes of achieving a higher price. So, your first offer should be something like £95,000. That is, it's low enough to reset their expectations, but it's high enough to be taken seriously. It's a fine balance.

Optional extra: Establish a range

Voss also offers another technique that's useful here – establishing a range. You can allude to similar deals in the marketplace to establish a "ballpark" around what the property might be worth. For example, you might say 'Based on my research, other one-bedroom apartments in this block have sold for between £85,000 and £98,000 in the past year'. It's even better if you can support this with data.

In this way, using a range can help you get your point across without getting the other party too defensive. It also gives the agent a way of explaining and justifying your low-ball offer to the seller. However, if you do use a range (and it's a good idea to do so) you should expect them to come in at the most favourable end of the range from their perspective. That is, at the high end for the seller.

Research shows that people who are presented with extreme anchors unconsciously adjust their expectations in the direction of the opening number.

Many people even jump straight to their price limit in this scenario. Unlock the potential for a deal by using an extreme anchor to bend their reality.

Negotiation Tip # 5 – Explain your offer

One of the biggest obstacles to overcome in a property negotiation is getting the agent onside. Because there's almost no direct contact between the buyer and the seller, you're relying on the agent to put forward your offer in the best light. The agent can do this in a cursory way, without giving it much weight. Or they can get behind your offer in a way that the seller is much more likely to accept.

The agent will want to reach a deal – after all, they don't get paid until the property is sold. But a low-ball offer will likely need a good deal of explanation. There's also a credibility point here for the agent too, as they likely advised the seller on the asking price in the first place. One of the secrets to successful property negotiations therefore is learning how to explain your offer.

How to explain your offer

The best strategy for getting the agent onboard is to explain any offer you put forward. You can do this in a number of different ways. For example, you could use a sales schedule to present your research on what similar properties have sold for in the same block. This can help to support your assessment of the property's current market value. You can also combine this with a range, as discussed above.

In fact, you can use any of the techniques we discussed in our chapter on valuing residential property to support your position. If you're flipping a property, you could present an estimate of what the property will likely be worth after all the work is done, along with your assessment of the cost of the works, to justify the price you're prepared to pay. You can use the arguments around under-rented or over-rented properties to support smaller adjustments to the price. In addition, you can also muddy the waters a bit by talking about transaction costs.

Personally, I've never had much success justifying offers using my personal investment criteria. That is, presenting a calculation of the ROI or capitalisation rate I hope to achieve has never worked for me. As such, I suggest sticking to market value as the best way to explain your offer to the agent, either using direct market comparables or indirectly using a cost-of-refurbishment type calculation.

You should aim for as simple an explanation as possible, as the agent will need to understand this and present this to the seller. In short, try not to overcomplicate things. This tip might be the single most important thing you can do to increase your chances of success.

Negotiation Tip # 6 – Try Ackerman bargaining

Back at FBI negotiation training, Voss learned a bargaining system he still uses to this day. And he swears by it. He calls it the Ackerman bargaining model, because it came from a fellow negotiator named Mike Ackerman. It's a very effective offer-counteroffer method that's much better than the usual lacklustre, meet-in-the-middle haggling dynamic. It's easy-to-remember and it has five steps. Let's look at how it works.

1. Set your target price (your goal)
2. Set your first offer at 86% of your target price
3. Calculate three raises (94%, 98% and 100% of your target)
4. The final offer should use a non-rounded number
5. On your final offer, throw in a non-monetary item

The genius of this system is it incorporates a range of psychological tactics – reciprocity, extreme anchors, etc – without you needing to think about them. I've changed the percentages slightly (Voss uses 65%, 85%, 95% and 100%) as Voss's system is a little extreme for a property negotiation. In my view, offering £65,000 for a property worth £100,000 is more likely to cause offence than bring you closer to a deal.

A note on the percentages themselves

If you look closely, Ackerman's original system works off incremental deductions of 0%, 5%, 10% and 20% from the final target price. That is, if we look at the offers in reverse order, we get the following:

- our last offer has a deduction of 0% applied (we offer 100%)
- the next-to-last offer has a deduction of 5% (we offer 95%)

- the second offer has a deduction of 15% (5% plus 10%)
- our first offer has a deduction of 35% (5% plus 10% plus 20%)

The size of the incremental deduction doubles in size each time and they're added together in a cumulative fashion to get the overall deductions of 0%, 5%, 15%, and 35% from the target price.

In the system above, I have proposed using increments of 0%, 2%, 4% and 8%. Again, these increments double each time, preserving the "closing in on the final offer" dynamic of Ackerman's original system. However, the overall deductions of 0%, 2%, 6% and 14% from the final target price are much more palatable from a property negotiation perspective and are less likely to cause offence.

Now that you know how to construct one, invent your own Ackerman system. In my experience, increments of 1%, 2%, and 4% (that is, offer percentages of 100%, 99%, 97% and 93% in reverse order) can also work well if the range for price negotiation is a little bit narrower and the buyer and seller are closer in their views.

Let's look at a simple example

Let's take our example from above. Suppose you're not prepared to pay more than £102,500 for the property based on your rental yield calculations.

Your first offer of £88,000 (86% × £102,500 rounded down to the nearest £1,000) will set an extreme anchor. It's a big slap in the face that might bring your counterpart right to their price limit. It will induce a flight-or-fight type reaction in all but the most experienced of negotiators. It'll likely get a very swift "No", but it will have served its purpose of resetting the seller's expectations.

Our second and third offers will be £96,000 (94% × £102,500 rounded down to the nearest £1,000) and £100,250 (98% × £102,500 rounded down to the nearest £250). You're going to drop these offers in sparingly after the counterpart has made another offer on their side and after you've used the dialogue to explore their other needs and interests a little bit further. These concessions will make the seller feel better about the bargaining process. They will feel that they've pushed hard to get your best price out of you. You are, in effect, giving them a win.

Making your final offer

Our final offer of £102,450 (calculated as 100% of £102,500 with £50 taken off) is purposefully unrounded. The unrounded number will add credibility and make it look like we've been pushed to our limit. We'll also throw in a non-monetary item too. This will signal that we're at our walkaway point (without ever saying so) and that we're really trying hard to make the deal work. Be creative – offer them £100 of John Lewis vouchers, a set of collectible gold coins, or perhaps a set of dining plates for their new home. It doesn't matter what you offer, as the seller probably won't want it anyway. It will, however, be seen as compelling and as a gesture of good faith in the interests of getting a deal done.

Voss also swears by using non-round numbers like £102,451 for your final offer. I've never been able to bring myself to go this far, but maybe you could give it a go? If it works, do drop me a line.

Negotiation Tip # 7 – Pivot to non-monetary terms

There's more to a negotiation than price. And when we forget this, we leave money on the table. People get fixated on the "How much?" and this can lead them to take a series of arbitrary positions wrapped up with their emotional views of fairness and pride.

You can take the focus off price by pivoting to non-monetary terms. In any property deal, there are a truck load of other things that can be used as bargaining chips. For example, there is the timeline for the move, the fixtures and fittings that are included, whether the property gets a clean beforehand, etc. Your lawyers will probably obsess over a range of smaller "deal risk" points. This will include things like which party pays for any under or overpayment of a service charge in a prior period when the seller was still the owner. You can add these into the mix too.

Example from a recent deal

On one recent deal, we'd reached our limit on price, but we still weren't quite at a deal. So, we decided to pivot to other terms. We knew the seller was a single guy who was selling his flat so that he could buy a larger house. The seller was a designer and he had great taste in furniture. The apartment itself was nicely furnished and we felt we could leave all his furniture in place and it would add value in the rental process. We decided to offer two things that we guessed he might value.

- We offered the seller the choice of completion date. We said we were okay to complete on whatever timescale worked best for him. The agent had told us he'd only just put the apartment on the market and he hadn't yet found a house. So, we gave him the time and space he needed to do this. We also gave him the chance to lock in a deal and get some certainty on his financial position before he started looking.

- We offered the seller £2,500 for chattels (that is, the existing furniture, washing machine, etc). We'd taken some good photos during the viewing process, and we used these to cost out what the existing furniture might have set him back. We offered 75% of the original price, as all the furniture was in good condition. And when we put this forward, we pitched it as £2,500 to help him furnish his new house.

We're not sure which of these two things sealed the deal for us, but the seller gave us a "Yes" and we completed three months later.

Negotiation Tip # 8 – Understand leverage

If you've ever watched 24, the hit US TV series starring Kiefer Sutherland, then you'll know all about leverage.

Leverage is the ability to inflict a loss or withhold a gain. The theory goes that if we can discover where our counterpart hopes to gain and what they fear losing, then we'll be able to create leverage over the other side's decisions. There are three kinds of leverage.

Positive leverage

This is your ability to provide things your counterpart wants.

In a property negotiation, positive leverage could be a movement on price or on one of the non-monetary terms discussed above. Here, you're trying to work out what your counterpart values. You should try to help your counterpart get what they want.

Negative leverage

This is your ability to make your counterpart suffer.

In a property deal, there are probably limited opportunities to use this type of leverage. Mild examples could include stalling for time when your counterpart is burning cash, e.g. with a vacant property, or being pedantic on legal points, e.g. if you require your counterpart to register a title with the land registry when it's not a formal requirement. Use this type of leverage carefully, as threats, even mild one, can be toxic and they can kill a deal.

Normative leverage

This is using the other party's "norms" to advance your position.

Every party has a set of rules and a moral framework. You can use these to present your offer in the best possible light or to highlight inconsistencies between their beliefs and actions. No one likes to look like a hypocrite. For example, if your counterpart says they won't sell the property for less than the market value, you can frame your desired price within the context of a market valuation. Think of this as negotiation Tai Chi, using your counterpart's energy against them.

There's so much to say on this topic that we can't possibly cover it all here. For more on how to use leverage, read Chapter Ten from Voss's book. It really is rather good.

Negotiation Tip # 9 – The waiting game

Our next to last tip is a simple one. Making your counterpart wait before you make your next move can work wonders. Waiting can help your extreme anchor work its magic on their subconscious. It can give your counterpart the time they need to come to terms with the idea that they won't get top dollar. It can also make you look like you're working hard in the background on a revised offer.

How long you wait will depend on the situation. Oftentimes, I'll leave it a couple of days after my extreme anchor offer is rejected before I put in a higher offer. I'll thank the agent for putting the offer forward and say that my partner and I will need to discuss whether we're prepared to increase our offer at all. Then I'll leave it a couple of days with no contact and let the idea of selling at a cheaper price really sink in.

You can experiment with different timings here. I tend to find that waiting a week or so between offers works quite well in the middle phase of a negotiation. Any longer and the deal kind of loses focus and energy. Towards the end of a negotiation, picking up the pace works well to try to seal the deal.

Negotiation Tip # 10 – The silent partner

Our final negotiation tip is called the silent partner. When I'm talking with agents, I'll often use my 'investment partner' as the excuse for needing additional time to consider the seller's counter-offer or the attractiveness of a revised deal. I do actually have a partner I discuss deals with, but it doesn't matter if you're going it alone. Your cat or your dog could be your partner, it really doesn't matter.

Use the silent partner technique to avoid making a decision there and then and to buy you time to properly consider your next move.

In conclusion

That brings us to the end of our chapter on property negotiations. I hope you've enjoyed this chapter and that you're keen to try out some of these techniques on your next deal. Adopt a learning mindset here and you won't go far wrong.

As a final comment, I want to remind you that there really is no secret sauce or button that you can press to get a deal done on your terms. Property negotiation is hard, and it's made even harder by the fact that there's an agent in the middle and because there's no direct contact between the buyer and seller. You'll need to work hard to uncover what's important to the seller and get creative.

You might also find that a little bit of cheekiness goes a long way. That's my 'cheeky bonus tip', the one I promised at the start to keep you reading. A cheeky line like 'I think we're almost there, what else can the seller offer to get the deal over the line?' can work wonders in sealing a deal. In the UK, we like a bit of cheekiness – why not use that sense of humour to help you unlock some value.

Part Two

Managing your property portfolio

Chapter 6

Accounting for property investors

You have to know accounting. It's the language of practical business life.

–Charlie Munger

Financial accounting is often called the language of business. It's the language that managers use to communicate a firm's financial and economic performance to lenders and investors. It's also the language that property investors need to speak to understand the performance of their portfolio. Nobody managing a large portfolio can afford financial illiteracy.

Whether you're just starting out in property or whether you've been doing this for some time but never really gotten to grips with the numbers side of things doesn't matter. This chapter will teach you the language of business. It will teach you the accounting fundamentals and terminology you need to interpret a set of financial statements. It will help you learn the business thinking and ideas you need to diagnose your property problems and improve your decisions.

This introduction to accounting should be read before the rest of the chapters in Part Two. However, if you're a qualified accountant or if you're extremely numbers-savvy you could consider skipping this session. I'll leave this up to you to decide.

Some important definitions

Like any technical field, financial accounting has its own vocabulary. First, we're going to run through some of the terminology and basic definitions you need to know before we delve a bit deeper.

Asset

This is anything that's owned by the business and which can be used to generate profits. Assets include things like property and land, machinery, vehicles, cash in the bank, inventory or stock.

Liability

This is anything that's owed by the business to a third party. Typical liabilities are things like loans, an overdrawn bank account, and any money you owe to a supplier for goods bought on credit.

Capital

This is a special type of liability of the business. It's the amount that the owner has invested in the business to get the business up and running. The business owes this back to the owner.

When a business is set up as a limited company, we sometimes call this the 'owner's equity' instead of capital.

Revenue

This is the income generated from the normal business operations. It is the top line income figure from which costs are subtracted to determine the profit the business has made.

Expense

This is any cost incurred by the business. Expenses can include everything from lighting and heating, staff wages and salaries, postage and packaging, advertising and sales promotions, etc.

Profit

This is the financial gain realised by a business when the revenue it generates exceeds its expenses. When the expenses of a business exceed its revenue, the business has instead generated a loss.

If you pick up an accounting textbook, you'll likely get more technical and esoteric definitions. But I've tried to keep these definitions simple and easy-to-understand.

The main financial statements

Let's look at the main financial statements we'll be dealing with in the analysis of our property business.

The balance sheet

The balance sheet is also known as the statement of financial position. It reports the value of a business's assets, liabilities and capital (i.e. owner's equity) at a specific point in time. Often this is at the start or end of a business's financial year.

The balance sheet is therefore a snapshot of what a business owns and owes. It also tells us the amount invested by the owners of the business and what the business owes back to them.

The statement of profit and loss

The statement of profit and loss is also known as the income statement. It reports the revenues, expenses, and the profit or loss in a specific period. Often this is over the course of a business's financial year or perhaps a particular quarter or half year.

The statement of profit and loss (or P&L for short) therefore tells us whether the business has been able to generate a profit.

Other financial statements

There are number of other financial statements you might find in a typical set of accounts. The cash flow statement shows the cash movements into and out of a business over the year. You might also see a statement of changes in equity, which shows how the capital or owner's equity has moved over the course of a year. We won't consider these other financial statements in detail here.

Fundamental accounting concepts

Next, we're going to look at five fundamental accounting concepts. These concepts underpin everything that goes on in accounting. You'll need to understand these before we can get to grips with some example financial statements.

(1) The separate entity principle

This fundamental accounting principle says that a business should be treated as separate and distinct from its owner.

If the owner of a business bought an asset for their personal use, the asset is not the property of the business. Likewise, if the business bought an asset, the asset is not the property of the owner. This principle also leads to the definition of capital we saw above. That is, when the owner injects money into the business, this is a liability of the business that needs to be repaid.

(2) The dual effect principle

The dual effect principle is the foundation of accounting. It states that every transaction has two financial effects.

Let's look at how this applies to a few simple transactions. Suppose David is the owner of a small retail business. He injects £10,000 into the new business to get it going. This injection of monies has had two financial effects:

Effect 1 – The business now has £10,000 in its bank account. This is an asset of the business worth £10,000.

Effect 2 – The business now owes David £10,000. This is a liability of the business, i.e. capital has increased by £10,000.

David then uses £5,000 of the money in the business bank account to buy stock for his shop. The two financial effects are:

Effect 1 – The business now has £5,000 of stock. This is an asset of the business worth £5,000.

Effect 2 – The business has £5,000 less cash in its bank account. That is, the assets held in cash have decreased by £5,000.

In the course of business, David sells this stock to its customers generating £6,000 of cash sales for the business.

Effect 1 – The business has £6,000 more in its bank account. This is an asset of the business.

Effect 2 – The stock (an asset) has decreased by £5,000. The shop has also generated £1,000 profit, which it now owes to David.

In this manner, every transaction that takes place affects two items in the accounts of a business. Understanding this is the first step to being able to record transactions in the accounting records.

(3) The accounting equation

The accounting equation is the foundation of the double entry bookkeeping system. The equation says that if we add up all the assets of the business and subtract off all its liabilities, what's left over is the capital, i.e. the owner's equity.

$$Assets - Liabilities = Capital$$

or

$$Net\ Assets = (Assets - Liabilities) = Capital$$

This equation can used at a particular point in time to work out the capital or owner's equity using the information on the balance sheet. The equation also provides the link between the balance sheet and the statement of profit and loss.

The profit generated over a period is equal to the change in capital or owner's equity, which in turn is equal to the change in net assets.

(4) The accruals concept

Accountants love the accruals concept. It's the concept that turns accounting from a simple spectator sport of watching the cash into a full-on contact sport. Okay, that might be overdoing it a little, but you get the idea.

The accruals concept states that revenue and expenses should be recognised in the period when they're earned or incurred. That is, we don't care when the cash actually changes hands, we only care about the date of the transaction itself.

A simple example

Let's take a simple example. Suppose that you buy some goods on credit from a supplier two weeks before your financial year ends on 31 March 2020. The supplier sends you the goods the next day along with an invoice requiring you to pay within 30 days. You pay the supplier 30 days later, two weeks after the end of the financial year. Now let's look at the accounting for this transaction.

Using accruals accounting, the expense of buying the goods is said to occur at the date the transaction is struck, i.e. when the supplier ships the products and sends you the invoice. In the accounts, we book the expense at this date, and we also create a short-term liability, a trade payable, which sits on our balance sheet at the end of the year as a debt we still need to pay.

In this example, using accruals accounting means the expense was recognised in the financial year ending 31 March 2020. If we had used cash accounting instead, we would have booked the expense in the following year when the invoice was actually paid.

Whether you're allowed to use cash or accruals accounting will depend on how your business is set up legally and the rules and regulations which govern the accounting. You should speak to your accountant about this if you're in any doubt.

(5) Revenue expenditure vs capital expenditure

Whatever type of activity the business is engaged in, it's important to distinguish between two different types of expenditure.

Revenue expenditure

Firstly, let's look at revenue expenditure. This is any spending on the day-to-day running expenses of a business. Examples include spending on utilities like gas and electricity, rent and rates, postage and packaging, etc. It also includes any expenses incurred on the repair and maintenance of longer-term assets, e.g. like buildings, machinery and vehicles.

Revenue expenditure is recognised in the accounting records of a business when it's incurred.

Capital expenditure

Secondly, let's look at capital expenditure. Capital expenditure is spending on the acquisition or improvement of longer-term assets, e.g. like buildings, machinery, vehicles. Examples would include buying a property, a new piece of machinery, or perhaps replacing single-glazed windows with double-glazed windows.

Capital expenditure is not recognised immediately in the accounts. Instead, it's recognised bit-by-bit over the useful lifetime of the asset, e.g. the cost of a new vehicle might be spread over five to ten years. This smoothing out of the cost is called depreciation.

These five fundamental accounting concepts form the basis of all modern accounting systems. There are different rules for different businesses and for different business set-ups. However, they're all based broadly on these five principles.

A set of proforma financial statements

Armed with our new accounting knowledge and definitions, we're going to look at a set of proforma financial statements for a property investment business. These statements would be typical for a business engaged in buy-to-let property investment.

No doubt this was the type of thing you hoped to find when you bought this book, scanned the contents page, and saw a chapter on accounting. So, let's jump right in.

One thing to note in advance is that when accountants put brackets around a number it means it's a negative number. I'll make use of this convention in the figures and tables I present below.

A proforma profit and loss

The table on the following page sets out a proforma P&L for a fictitious property investment company we'll call Green Leaf Properties Limited. We're going to work through each of the lines in the P&L in turn and explain what each one means and how it was calculated.

(a) Revenue

For a property investment business, the revenue line will mainly consist of the rental income from your buy-to-let properties. If you provide any other services to your tenants, e.g. cleaning services, you should make sure to include these revenues here too.

In our example accounts, the total rental income received for the financial year ended 31 March 2020 was £21,600.

(b) Cost of sales

The cost of sales line tells us how much it costs a business to produce the goods or services it sells to its customers. This line only includes the costs directly associated with the production of the goods or services included in the revenue line.

For a property investment business, the cost of sales line will include any costs you can associate directly with one of your rental units. It includes all expenses associated with the upkeep of the rental properties and any costs related to letting out of the units. It's a good idea to separate these costs into categories so that you can track where the costs have been incurred.

- Ground rent and service charge – The cost of any ground rents payable to the freeholder of the property and for apartments the service charges paid to the management company.

Statement of profit and loss for the year ended 31 March 2020

		£	£
Revenue	(a)		21,600
Less: Cost of sales	(b)		
- Ground rent and service charge		2,850	
- Legal and professional fees		2,592	
- Premises insurance		840	
- Property repairs and maintenance		220	
- Cost of services provided		218	
		6,720	
			(6,720)
Gross profit/(loss)	(c)=(a)-(b)		14,880
Less: Administrative expenses	(d)		
- Audit and accountancy fees		900	
- Bank fees and charges		68	
- Legal and professional fees		250	
- Insurance		120	
- Telephone		192	
- Payroll expenses		0	
- Rent and rates		0	
- Lighting and heating		0	
- Sundry expenses		24	
- Depreciation		1,000	
		2,554	
			(2,554)
Operating profit/(loss)	(e)=(c)-(d)		12,326
Less: Finance costs	(f)		
- Interest paid		7,164	
- Finance charges		0	
		7,164	
			(7,164)
Profit/(loss) before taxation	(g)=(e)-(f)		5,162

- Legal and professional fees – This line includes any legal and professional fees you've incurred in renting out a property. For example, this includes property management fees, any legal fees associated with a tenant eviction, etc.

- Premises insurance – You can include the cost of buildings insurance and other types of landlord's insurance here.

- Property repairs and maintenance – This includes property repairs and other expenses on maintenance and upkeep.

- Cost of services provided – The costs associated with any additional services provided to the tenant, e.g. a cleaning service. I would also include the cost of utilities, e.g. council tax and electricity, incurred in a void period here too.

In the above example, the total cost of sales for the financial year ended 31 March 2020 was £6,720. We get this by summing up all the line items discussed above.

(c) Gross profit or loss

This is the profit a business makes after deducting the costs associated with making and selling its products and services. The gross profit or loss is calculated by subtracting the cost of sales from the top line revenue figure.

In the example above, Green Leaf Properties made a gross profit for the financial year ended 31 March 2020 of £14,880.

(d) Administrative expenses

Administrative expenses are the expenses of a business which are not directly tied to the goods and services sold to its customers. These expenses are related to the business as a whole. A business will always incur some level of administrative expenses.

For a property investment company, administrative expenses could include bank charges, legal or professional fees which are not related to the rental of a specific property, accountancy fees, or perhaps the cost of insurance relating to the business as a whole, e.g. directors' and officers' liability insurance. If you have an office or a head office, this could also include rent, rates, lighting and heating.

The proforma P&L above lists out a variety of expenses. Apart from the last two, most of these are self-explanatory.

- Sundry expenses – Any other small, infrequent expenses. This line will likely include the combined total of several expense accounts that have small balances. If such expenses reoccur, a new expenses type should be added.

- Depreciation – The depreciation expense, which we discussed briefly above, is the accounting charge for larger, capital expenditure items. The cost of these larger items is recognised gradually over the useful economic life of the asset.

For a property investment business, depreciation expenses are most likely to be in relation to assets like fixtures and fittings. This would include, for example, the cost of furniture, larger appliances, and things like rugs and artwork.

In our example, Green Leaf Properties incurred administrative expenses of £2,554 for its financial year ended 31 March 2020.

(e) Operating profit or loss

This is the profit or loss that a business makes after deducting the administrative costs from the gross profit or loss figure. Its calculated before the deduction of finance costs and taxes, which we'll come to in just a moment.

Looking at our example, Green Leaf Properties made an operating profit of £12,326 for this financial year.

(f) Finance costs

Finance costs include interest paid to lenders on loans and mortgages and interest on bank overdraft facilities. It also includes any other costs incurred by the business while borrowing funds. The latter are often labelled as finance charges under a separate line item.

For a property investment business, interest paid will mainly include mortgage interest expenses. The finance charges line could, for example, include mortgage valuation fees or any arrangement fees incurred while taking out a new mortgage or on refinancing.

In our example accounts for Green Leaf Properties, the finance costs for the financial year ended 31 March 2020 were £7,164.

(g) Profit or loss before taxation

Finally, we calculate the profit or loss before taxation by subtracting the finance costs from the operating profit or loss.

For the financial year ended 31 March 2020, Green Leaf Properties achieved a profit before tax of £5,162.

A proforma balance sheet

The table on the next page sets out a proforma balance sheet for Green Leaf Properties Limited. As we did for the P&L, we're going to work through each line in turn and explain what each one means.

(i) Non-current assets

Our balance sheet kicks off with a list of non-current assets owned by the business. Non-current assets, sometimes called fixed assets, are longer term assets which cannot be converted into cash quickly. They are likely to be held by the business for more than a year. Typical examples include property, machinery and equipment, and vehicles.

For a property investment business, you'll likely have two main types of non-current assets on your balance sheet.

Investment properties

This is the value of your investment properties themselves. Under typical accounting rules, the properties need to be valued at fair value. Just after purchasing a property, the amount you show will be the total purchase cost (including all purchase expenses, e.g. stamp duty, legal fees, etc). Over time, you may need to adjust this figure.

Fixtures and fittings

This is the value of any fixtures and fittings, e.g. the cost of furniture, larger appliances and things like rugs and artwork. The amount you recognise on the balance sheet is set equal to the original purchase cost less the accumulated value of depreciation expensed to the P&L.

In the example above, Green Leaf Properties owned investment properties worth £300,000 and fixtures and fittings worth £4,000 as at 31 March 2020. Note that the fixtures and fittings themselves were valued as the original cost of £5,000 less accumulated depreciation of £1,000, what's known as the carrying value of the asset.

(ii) Current assets

Current assets are assets that can easily be converted into cash. They are likely to be converted into cash within one year. Typical examples of current assets include inventory or stock, cash in the bank, and trade receivables. The trade receivables line is the money owed to the business by its customers where goods or services have been delivered but not yet paid for, i.e. sales on credit.

Prepayments are also known as prepaid expenses. These are any expenses that you've paid in advance, but you've not yet used. For example, suppose you've paid a solicitor £300 as a deposit for legal services they've not yet provided. Effectively the solicitor owes you £300 of legal services that they'll need to provide in the future. This is an asset on the balance sheet.

In our example, Green Leaf Properties had £2,800 of current assets in total at the 31 March 2020 balance sheet date. This is made up of £2,500 of cash in the business bank account and a £300 prepayment.

(iii) Current liabilities

Current liabilities are short term liabilities that are due for payment in the next year. Typical examples include an overdrawn bank account and trade payables. The trade payables line is money owed by the business to its suppliers where the goods or services have been delivered but not yet paid for, i.e. purchases on credit.

Statement of financial position as at 31 March 2020

		£	£
Non-current assets	(i)		
- Investment properties		300,000	
- Fixtures and fittings		4,000	
		304,000	
			304,000
Current assets	(ii)		
- Inventory		0	
- Trade receivables		0	
- Prepayments		300	
- Cash at bank		2,500	
		2,800	
Current liabilities	(iii)		
- Trade payables		250	
- Accruals		900	
		1,150	
Net current assets	(iv)=(ii)-(iii)		1,650
Total assets less current liabilities	(v)=(i)+(iv)		305,650
Non-current liabilities	(vi)		
- Bank loan		220,000	
		220,000	
			(220,000)
Net assets	(vii)=(v)-(vi)		85,650
Capital	(viii)		
- Capital introduced by owners		70,000	
- Sum of prior profits/(losses)		5,488	
- Increase in revaluation reserve		5,000	
- Current year profit/(loss)		5,162	
		85,650	
Capital at end of year			85,650

Accruals are also known as accrued expenses. They are expenses the business has incurred, but which have not been invoiced. For example, suppose you've used £250 of water and heating services, but you've not yet received an invoice for these services. You still owe £250 to the utility company for these services, and this sits on the balance sheet as a liability.

In our example, Green Leaf Properties had £1,150 of current liabilities on its balance sheet as at the 31 March 2020. This is made up of £250 of trade payables and £900 of accruals.

(iv) Net current assets

Net current assets is the total of all current assets less the total of all current liabilities. There should be a positive amount of net current assets on hand, as this means there are enough short term "cash-like" assets to meet the short term liabilities.

As at the 31 March 2020 balance sheet date, Green Leaf Properties had net current assets of £1,650.

(v) Total assets less current liabilities

This line is calculated by adding the value of the business's non-current assets to the net current assets.

For Green Leaf Properties, we calculate this by adding the £304,000 of non-current assets to £1,650 of net current assets.

(vi) Non-current liabilities

The non-current liabilities are the long-term liabilities or long-term debts of a business. This includes any long-term liabilities that will fall due after one year. Typical examples include long-term loans, bonds payable, or perhaps deferred tax liabilities.

For a property investment business, the main non-current liabilities are likely to be the outstanding mortgage balances.

In our example, Green Leaf Properties had outstanding mortgage debts of £220,000 on its balance sheet at 31 March 2020.

(vii) Net assets

The net assets of the business are calculated as the total assets less total liabilities.

In our example, Green Leaf Properties had net assets of £85,650 as at 31 March 2020. This is calculated by subtracting the long-term mortgage debt of £220,000 from £305,650, the sum of all the assets less the current liabilities.

(viii) Capital

We can see from the accounting equation section above that net assets, i.e. total assets less total liabilities, is equal to capital or owner's equity. The final section of the balance sheet then provides a reconciliation of the capital at the start and end of the year.

For Green Leaf Properties, the capital or owner's equity at the start of the year was £75,488. The owners have introduced capital of £70,000 into the business which the business owes back to them. In addition, the cumulative sum of the profits and losses made by the business in all financial years prior to the current year was £5,488. The business also owes these accumulated profits back to the owners. So, we add these two figures together to find the total capital or owner's equity at the start of the year of £75,488.

Over the course of this financial year ended 31 March 2020, the business made a further £5,162 profit. These profits increase the capital balance due to the owners. Furthermore, one of the properties owned by the business increased in value by £5,000 over the course of the year. This increase in the capital value of a property doesn't get recognised in the P&L, but it does increase the capital balance due back to the owners. In the reconciliation, we label this as an increase in the *revaluation reserve*. Taken together, if we add the current year's profit of £5,162 and the increase in the property value of £5,000 to the capital at the start of the year of £75,488, we calculate the capital at the end of the year as £85,650.

If we've calculated our balance sheet and our P&L correctly, then the capital at the end of the year will be equal to the net assets of the business. Hence, the balance sheet – well, balances. In this way, the balance sheet and P&L are always linked.

Frequently asked accounting questions

Now that we've looked at some proforma financial statements, it's worth running through some FAQs. These are some of the questions I commonly see posted on the property forums and which I thought I could usefully answer in one place.

Q1. When I set up a limited company, how do I account for my initial injection of monies to the business?

If you've set up your own small, limited company in the UK, then you've likely also appointed yourself and/or your partner as Directors of the company. Whilst you could theoretically set up the initial injection of funds as *share capital* – that is, the capital of a company that comes from the issue of new shares, it is much simpler for you to loan the money to the company.

If you go down the loan route, the loan will be classified as a director's loan to the business. Because it's money the company owes back to you, it technically counts as a liability, rather than share capital or owner's equity, when recognised on the balance sheet. As such, it will normally sit as a short-term liability along with other current liabilities until it is repaid.

Your bookkeeper or property accountant can deal with the precise accounting entries for the loan. However, when it comes to analysis of your accounts and your investment returns, it's much better to treat directors' loan balances as akin to capital or owner's equity.

Q2. How does the P&L relate to the cash flows of a business?

If you're using the accruals accounting method, then the P&L will not be equal to the business's cash flow. This is because expenses will be recognised when they're incurred, rather than when the cash is paid out. Also, for larger capital expenses, e.g. spending on fixtures and fittings like furniture, the cash will be paid out on day one, but the cost of these items will be spread out over time as depreciation.

If you want an estimate of the cash flows of the business, then you could build this up directly from the entries in your bank account. Alternatively, you can estimate cash flow from the accounting entries in your P&L statement. It's a bit technical, so you may need to speak to your bookkeeper or property accountant if you need to do this.

If you're using accounting software, e.g. Xero or Quickbooks, these programs will provide a cash flow statement for you.

Q3. My business does flips and developments. How does the accounting for this type of business differ?

The accounting for property investors engaged in activities like flips, trading or property development is a whole different ball game. For a business that engages in flips, the revenue line is instead the sale of the refurbished properties and the cost of sales line is the cost of buying and refurbishing the property. It is therefore a different kind of business from property rentals.

If you're engaged in these types of activities, speak to your bookkeeper or property accountant about the accounting entries.

Q4. Do I need a bookkeeper or a property accountant?

The complexity of accounting for property investors will depend on the legal set up of the business, e.g. sole trader vs limited company.

If you've bought property in your personal name, then you're set up as a sole trader. You'll need to file a self-assessment tax return, but that's about it. If you're pretty numbers-savvy, then you might decide to go it alone and do the accounting yourself. However, even here I would recommend using an accountant. A property accountant will have strong knowledge of the tax rules and this knowledge will probably save you more in tax than the accountant will charge you for the accounting services.

If you've set up a limited company, then you'll almost certainly want to appoint a bookkeeper and/or a property accountant. Limited companies need to file their financial statements and tax returns with Companies House each year. These accounts need to be prepared in accordance with the relevant accounting standards (e.g. UK GAAP) and with the requirements set out under UK legislation (e.g. the Companies Act 2006). Only a property accountant will really be able to help you with this.

In conclusion

That brings us to the end of our chapter on accounting for property investors. I hope you've enjoyed this chapter and that you're now one step closer to mastering your property books and financials. Before we move on, one word of warning.

This introduction and the proforma financial statements discussed here are provided for educational purposes only. You should speak to an accountant about your specific tax and accounting requirements. The rules around accounting for property investors depend on how your business is set up legally, e.g. as a sole trader, limited company, etc. They also vary depend on the activities your business carries out, e.g. buy-to-let, flips or property trading. If you're not an expert in this area, there's lots of potential to get this wrong, so you really ought to be working with a good accountant when you prepare your accounts and financial records.

With this introduction to accounting under our belt, we're going to move on to bigger and better things. Our next chapter will look at how to measure the returns you're achieving on your property portfolio. It builds on the concepts we've covered here and develops quantitative metrics that you can use to properly understand the returns on your property portfolio.

Chapter 7

How to measure your returns

Whatsoever a man soweth, that shall he also reap.

–The Bible

Our next chapter on property management is all about how to calculate property returns. I'm really excited about this one, as it combines two of my favourite things – property and accounting. Yes, I'm a bit of a geek, but that's a good thing, right? Well, it led me to write this book, so it can't be too much of a bad thing. I'll let you be the judge of that one though.

We're going to cover a range of metrics you can use to calculate property returns. Some of these will be metrics at the total portfolio level. These metrics will help you get to grips with the returns generated by your portfolio as a whole. Then we're going to look at some metrics you can use to judge the returns generated by individual properties in your portfolio. All in all, we'll cover the six areas I track at the portfolio level and five areas I track for the individual properties in my portfolio.

The real power of these metrics is in monitoring the performance of your portfolio over time. Here we're just going to look at the metrics themselves and how to calculate them for a single year. We'll do this to keep it simple. In practice though, you'll want to calculate these metrics for several years and monitor the trends over time. Towards the end of the chapter, I'll show you how you can calculate a multi-year average using a formula taken straight from the investment manager's playbook.

How to measure portfolio returns

The metrics you learn in this chapter will help you understand the returns you're achieving. Perhaps more importantly, they will give you an objective way to measure and monitor the performance of your portfolio over time. This will help you be honest with yourself about the impact of the decisions you've made in the past and help you make better ones in the future.

We're going to use our fictitious property investment business, Green Leaf Properties Limited, to illustrate with examples how to carry out each of the calculations. I'm going to carefully define each of the metrics I use and where relevant I'll also give you a formula.

Performance metrics at the total portfolio level

To start with, let's look at the metrics you'll want to track at the total portfolio level. Some of these are simple metrics that will help you keep track of whether you're hitting your wider property goals. Other metrics will require more detailed calculations.

The table on the following page sets out the figures, calculations and metrics for Green Leaf Properties Limited. The figures presented are consistent with those presented in the previous chapter. As such, you'll be able to see how to work through from the source P&L and balance sheet data we presented in the last chapter to the calculation of the overall return metrics that we'll use to track performance.

(a) Summary portfolio statistics

The performance metrics you use to track your portfolio over time should include some summary portfolio statistics. This could include, for example, the number of properties in your portfolio, the capital value of the properties on a combined basis, and the total revenue generated over the year.

Historical performance for the year ended 31 March 2020

	£	£
Statement of profit and loss		
Revenue		21,600
Less: Cost of sales		(6,720)
Gross profit/(loss)		14,880
Less: Administrative expenses		(2,554)
Operating profit/(loss)		12,326
Less: Finance costs		(7,164)
Profit/(loss) before taxation		5,162

Balance sheet	*31-Mar-19*	*31-Mar-20*
Non-current assets	300,000	304,000
Current assets	300	2,800
Total assets	300,300	306,800
Less: Current liabilities	(4,812)	(1,150)
Total assets less current liabilities	295,488	305,650
Less: Non-current liabilities	(220,000)	(220,000)
Net assets (owner's equity)	75,488	85,650

Performance metrics		
Number of properties	(a)	2
Value of the portfolio	(a)	£300,000
Revenue	(a)	£21,600
Gross profit margin	(b)	68.9%
Operating profit margin	(c)	57.1%
Administrative expenses ratio	(d)	11.8%
Return on capital employed (ROCE)	(e)	4.2%
Return on equity (ROE)	(f)	6.8%

The metrics you track should tie in with your wider property goals. For example, if you're aiming to grow your portfolio in size, you'll likely want to track both the number of properties you own and the total capital value of the properties. If you have set yourself a wealth target instead, you could include a metric around the total value of the equity you have accrued across all your properties.

In the example above, we can see that Green Leaf Properties owns two rental properties which are worth £300,000. These two rental properties generated a combined revenue of £21,600 in the financial year ended 31 March 2020.

(b) Gross profit margin

We calculate the gross profit margin by taking the gross profit and dividing this by the revenue.

$$Gross\ profit\ margin = \frac{Gross\ profit}{Revenue}$$

The gross profit margin tells us what percentage of the revenue generated is profit, after we've paid our cost of sales. A high gross profit margin tells us that our portfolio is generating strong returns and that our investments are profitable. A low gross profit margin could indicate that we've set our rents too low, had a high level of voids, or that our cost of sales has been high.

In the above example, Green Leaf Properties has a gross profit margin of 68.9%. This is calculated by taking the gross profit figure of £14,880 and dividing by the revenue figure of £21,600.

(c) Operating profit margin

The operating profit margin tells us how much profit a business makes on each pound of revenue after deducting all the expenses included within cost of sales and administrative expenses. It's calculated before any interest or tax expenses.

$$Operating\ profit\ margin = \frac{Operating\ profit}{Revenue}$$

A high operating profit margin again indicates that your portfolio is generating strong returns after all your key expenses are considered. A low margin indicates low rental income, high expenses, or both. You'll need to dig into this to find out why.

In the above example, Green Leaf Properties has an operating profit margin of 57.1%. This is calculated by taking the operating profit figure of £12,326 and dividing by the revenue of £21,600.

Note that operating profit is sometimes called net profit and this metric is then called the net profit margin. Knowing this will also help you if you ever go on Dragons' Den or Shark Tank. You know how those Dragons can get when someone fumbles the figures.

(d) Administrative expenses ratio

We calculate the administrative expenses ratio as follows.

$$Administrative\ expenses\ ratio = \frac{Administrative\ expenses}{Revenue}$$

For Green Leaf Properties, we take the administrative expenses of £2,554 and divide by the revenue figure of £21,600. This gives an administrative expenses ratio of 11.8%. Alternatively, we can calculate this ratio by subtracting the operating profit margin of 57.1% from the gross profit margin of 68.9%. This alternative method gives the same answer of 11.8% for this ratio.

The administrative expenses ratio tells us how much of our revenues are eaten up by our administrative or overhead expenses. Ideally, we want this ratio to be a low as possible. A low value tells us that we're running our business efficiently and that we are keeping our overhead expenses low.

For a property rental business, this ratio tends to decrease as the portfolio size increases, if we're managing our assets well.

(e) Return on capital employed (ROCE)

Our next profitability metric is return on capital employed (ROCE). ROCE is a measure of how well the business is generating profits from its full capital base or capital employed. It's worth pointing out that "capital" here means something slightly different in this context than it did in our previous chapter. This can cause some confusion to new property investors. Let's use some formulae to explain.

$$Return\ on\ capital\ employed\ (ROCE) = \frac{Operating\ profit}{Capital\ employed}$$

where capital employed is defined as

$$Capital\ employed = Total\ assets - Current\ liabilities$$

Rearranging this last formula gives us

$$= Total\ assets - (Total\ liabilities - Non\text{-}current\ liabilities)$$

$$= (Total\ assets - Total\ liabilities) + Non\text{-}current\ liabilities$$

Finally, we get the following

$$Capital\ employed = Net\ assets + Non\text{-}current\ liabilities$$

The first equation for capital employed above is the easiest way to calculate it. However, the last equation shows us that capital employed is defined here as the net assets (or owner's equity) plus non-current (or long-term) liabilities like bank loans. As such, capital employed is a measure of the total funding that the business has received from both the owners of the business and the lenders.

ROCE is frequently regarded as the best measure of a business's profitability. It indicates how successful a business has been in utilising the funding it has received to generate profits. In effect, it tells us how much profit has been made for each pound of funding the business has received from the owners and lenders combined.

An example calculation

You'll notice in the historical performance table above that I've added in the balance sheet position as at the 31 March 2019, i.e. the start of the financial year, as well as the position at 31 March 2020, the end of the financial year. This is because ROCE is normally calculated using the capital employed figure at the start of the financial year.

For Green Leaf Properties, we therefore take the operating profit of £12,326 and divide by the capital employed of £295,488 at the start of the financial year. This gives us a ROCE of 4.2%. In other words, the business has generated around £0.04 for every £1.00 of capital provided by the owners and banks combined.

Extension: Return on average capital employed (ROACE)

It's worth noting that this ratio is sometimes calculated using an average of the capital employed figure at the start and end of the financial year. This can give a better measure of profitability where the capital employed has moved a lot over the year. In this case, the metric is called the return on average capital employed (or ROACE) and the formula used to calculate it is as follows:

$$ROACE = \frac{Operating\ profit}{Average\ capital\ employed}$$

The average capital employed is calculated as the sum of the capital employed at the start of the year and the capital employed at the end of the year divided by 2, i.e. it's an estimate of the average capital employed over the course of the financial year.

For Green Leaf Properties, the capital employed is £295,488 at the start of the year end and £305,650 at the end of the year. The average capital employed is therefore (£295,488 + £305,650) ÷ 2 which equals £300,569. If we take the operating profit of £12,326 and divide by £300,569, this gives us a ROACE of 4.1%.

It doesn't matter which of these metrics you choose to use in your portfolio returns analysis. However, it is crucial that you keep this metric consistent over time. That way, you'll be able to spot the trends in your investment returns over time.

Note that another way to think about ROCE is that it tells us the profitability of the business if it were completely unlevered, i.e. if we owned 100% of all our rental properties. In this way, ROCE is a sort of capitalisation rate for your property portfolio as a whole.

(f) Return on equity

Return on equity (ROE) looks at the return earned by the owners of the business. For a business set up as a limited company, this is the return earned by the ordinary shareholders. For a sole trader, this will simply be the return earned by the owner.

$$Return\ on\ equity\ (ROE) = \frac{Profit\ before\ tax}{Net\ assets}$$

As for ROCE above, the convention is that we use the net assets or owner's equity at the start of the year for this calculation.

For Green Leaf Properties, therefore, we take the profit before tax of £5,162 and divide by the net assets or owner's equity of £75,488 at the start of the year. This gives us a ROCE of 6.8%. The business has generated c. £0.07 for every £1.00 of owner's equity.

There are other formulae you can use for ROE instead of the above. For example, some analysts prefer to use profit after tax in the formula above, as this is then based on the returns ultimately earned for the owners of the business. However, I prefer to use profit before tax. This is because the tax paid is a consequence of how you've set your business up, not how well you're managing your assets. For this reason, I prefer to use profit before tax in the above and leave the tax decisions for another day.

Extension: Return on average equity (ROAE)

Return on equity is sometimes calculated using an average of the net assets at the start and end of the financial year. Again, this can give a better measure of profitability where the owner's equity has moved a lot over the year. In this case, the metric is the called the return on average equity (ROAE) and the formula used is as follows:

$$Return\ on\ average\ equity\ (ROAE) = \frac{Profit\ before\ tax}{Average\ net\ assets}$$

The average net assets is calculated as the sum of the net assets at the start of the year and the net assets at the end of year divided by 2.

For Green Leaf Properties, net assets are £75,488 at the start of the year end and £85,650 at the end of the year. The average net asset figure is therefore (£75,488 + £85,650) ÷ 2 which equals £80,569. If we take the profit before tax figure of £5,162 and divide by the average net assets of £80,569, this gives us an ROAE of 6.4%. This figure is slightly lower than the ROE figure of 6.8% for the same period. This is because the average net assets increased over the year.

Again, I want to make a quick analogy here. ROE tells us about the profitability of the business after paying all its expenses, including interest on its borrowings. In this way, ROE is a sort of ROI measure for your property portfolio as a whole.

Adjustments for one-off items

When you're trying to understand the performance of your portfolio, there will sometimes be one-off costs or income items that you feel are distorting the underlying profitability figures. For example, you might have spent £1,000 on legal fees having a solicitor go through a number of auction legal packs on potential new property purchases. Even if no purchases were made, these costs will still have been recorded in your P&L expenses, e.g. within administrative expenses. As such, these costs will reduce your profitability metrics. However, they are speculative costs not related to running your core property rental business.

In this type of situation, it's okay (for your own analysis purposes, not for statutory accounting purposes) to make manual adjustments to the operating profit figure to remove the impact of these one-off items. For example, you could add back £1,000 to operating profit to remove the impact of these one-off legal costs and use the higher operating profit figure in your portfolio returns analysis.

These types of manual accounting adjustments are known as *quality of earnings* or *normalisation* adjustments. It's a totally valid thing to do if you're trying to look through the recorded figures and understand the profitability of the underlying property portfolio. However, because the adjustments you're making are subjective in nature, you need to make sure you don't take it too far. For example, if you do actually expect to incur some level of legal fees every year reviewing auction legal packs, i.e. if this is a core part of your business strategy, you should probably include something in your P&L for this type of expense after all.

It's all a matter of judgement. And remember, it's important to be honest with yourself. You'll learn more that way in the end.

Performance metrics at the individual property level

Now that we've looked at the metrics we can use at the total portfolio level, we're going to turn our attention to some property-by-property return metrics. That is, we're going to learn how to calculate property returns at the level required to understand the performance of each individual property in our portfolio.

The table opposite sets out figures, calculations and metrics for Green Leaf Properties Limited. Again, I've used figures that are consistent with those presented in the earlier part of this chapter and in the last chapter, so you'll be able to see where each of these figures comes from. We'll be able to look at these new metrics for each of the properties in Green Leaf's portfolio to work out which ones are performing the best and how this ties to the overall return metrics we've calculated in the earlier part of this chapter.

(i) Key property statistics

As we did at the overall portfolio level, the performance metrics we use to track individual properties over time should include some key statistics for each individual property. This could include the revenue generated, the increase in the value of the property experienced over the year, and the monthly profit generated by the property.

It's worth spending a couple of minutes explaining the calculation of the metrics that I've included in the table above.

- Revenue – This is simply the revenue generated by the property over the year. For Property A, our one-bedroom apartment, this was £9,000; for Property B, our two-bedroom apartment, this was £12,600.

Performance of individual properties for year ended 31 March 2020

	Admin £	Property A £	Property B £
P&L for year ended 31 March 2020			
Revenue	-	9,000	12,600
Less: Cost of sales	-	(3,078)	(3,642)
Gross profit/(loss)	-	5,922	8,958
Less: Administrative expenses	(1,554)	(400)	(600)
Operating profit/(loss)	(1,554)	5,522	8,358
Less: Finance costs	-	(3,072)	(4,092)
Profit/(loss) before taxation	(1,554)	2,450	4,266
Performance metrics			
Revenue	(i)	£9,000	£12,600
Profit per month	(i)	£204	£356
Increase in value of property	(i)	£5,000	-
Gross yield	(ii)	7.1%	7.3%
Capitalisation rate	(ii)	4.3%	4.8%
Return on investment (ROI)	(iii)	7.2%	9.3%
Capital growth (CG)	(iv)	14.7%	-
Total return (TR)	(v)	21.9%	9.3%

Notes on figures

Green Leaf Properties owns two properties which generated rental returns in the financial year ended 31 March 2020. Property A is a one-bedroom apartment in Manchester, whereas Property B is a two-bedroom apartment in Birmingham. The table above splits each of the lines in the P&L, i.e. revenue, cost of sales, etc, between the two properties. Administrative expenses that cannot be attributed to a property are shown in a separate column.

Balance sheet split between the individual properties

	Property A £	Property B £	Total £
Balance sheet as at 31 March 2019			
Non-current assets			
- Investment properties	125,000	170,000	295,000
- Fixtures and fittings	2,000	3,000	5,000
- Total non-current assets	127,000	173,000	300,000
Non-current liabilities			
- Bank loan	(93,000)	(127,000)	(220,000)
Equity in each property	34,000	46,000	80,000
Plus: Current assets			300
Less: Current liabilities			(4,812)
Net assets (owner's equity)			75,488
Balance sheet as at 31 March 2020			
Non-current assets			
- Investment properties	130,000	170,000	300,000
- Fixtures and fittings	1,600	2,400	4,000
- Total non-current assets	131,600	172,400	304,000
Non-current liabilities			
- Bank loan	(93,000)	(127,000)	(220,000)
Equity in each property	38,600	45,400	84,000
Plus: Current assets			2,800
Less: Current liabilities			(1,150)
Net assets (owner's equity)			85,650

Notes on figures

The table above presents a breakdown of the balance sheet between the two properties and a bridge to the earlier figures.

- Profit per month – I like to get a measure of the monthly profit generated by each property before tax. I calculate this by taking the profit before tax figure for each property and dividing through by 12. Property A generated £204 of profit per month before tax (£2,450 ÷ 12) and Property B made £356 of profit per month before tax (£4,266 ÷ 12).

- Increase in value of the property – In the second of the two tables, you can see a summary of the balance sheet at the start and end of the financial year. We calculate the increase in value of the property over the year as the difference in the value of the investment property at the start and end of the year. This was £5,000 for Property A and nil for Property B.

Once again, the metrics you decide to track should tie in with your property goals. For example, if you're aiming to grow your wealth, you could include a metric around the equity you have in each property.

(ii) Gross yield and capitalisation rate

We've covered gross yield and capitalisation rate in Chapter One, but I'll recap briefly here. Gross yield is a simple headline measure of the return on a property. In general, we calculate gross yield using the following formula:

$$Gross\ yield = \frac{Rental\ income}{Purchase\ price}$$

Using our figures in the table, we take the revenue generated by the property and use this in place of the rental income. Then, we divide this by the sum of the value of the property and the value of the fixtures and fittings at the start of the financial year. This sum tells us the combined worth of the investment property and the fixtures and fittings, both of which we have used to generate the revenue. Note that we don't use the original purchase price here, we use a figure that tells us what the property is worth now. That's because the amount the property is worth will change over time, and so to accurately assess the yield we need to use an up-to-date figure for the value of the property. This is a modification of the gross yield formula that's better suited to assessing the ongoing return a property is making.

For Green Leaf Properties, we calculate the gross yield for Property A to be 7.1% (as £9,000 ÷ £127,000) and we calculate the gross yield for Property B to be 7.3% (calculated as £12,600 ÷ £173,000).

The capitalisation rate

Next, we're going to take a look at the capitalisation rate. In general, we calculate the capitalisation rate using the following formula:

$$Cap\ rate = \frac{Net\ operating\ profit}{Purchase\ price}$$

Using the figures in our table, we take the operating profit generated by the property and divide this by the sum of the value of the property and the value of the fixtures and fittings at the start of the financial year. We do this for the same reasons set out above, and again this is a modification of the basic formula for capitalisation rate that's better suited to assessing the return generated by the property over time.

For Green Leaf Properties, we calculate the capitalisation rate for Property A to be 4.3% (calculated as £5,522 ÷ £127,000) and we calculate the capitalisation rate for Property B to be 4.8% (calculated as £8,358 ÷ £173,000).

From these metrics, we can see that Property B had a higher gross yield and a higher capitalisation rate this financial year than Property A. The capitalisation rate is the better yield metric here, as it takes into account property expenses too, not just revenue. It shows us the yield we would have generated if we owned the property outright with no mortgage financing.

What can you read into these calculations?

We've covered gross yield and capitalisation rate in some detail in our earlier chapters on how to assess a property deal.

However, it's worth noting that these yield metrics will also move around with changes in property prices. For example, if one of your properties experiences strong capital growth, this will decrease the capitalisation rate by increasing the "purchase price" input into the formula above. As such, gross yields and capitalisation rates will sometimes fall in areas which have achieved strong capital growth. In this type of situation, you'll naturally be asking yourself whether now is a good time to sell the property and lock in the gain or whether you should continue to hold the property for the rental yield.

Also, it's worth saying that rather than placing too much weight on one particular year, you should make sure to look at the averages over several years. We'll come back to this point later and I'll show you how to calculate a proper average.

(iii) Return on investment (ROI)

Next in our list of return metrics is return on investment (or ROI). Again, we've covered this in an earlier chapter, but I'll recap here as we're going to use a slight variation on the usual ROI formula.

$$Return\ on\ investment\ (ROI) = \frac{Profit\ before\ tax}{Equity\ in\ property}$$

That is, to calculate our ROI we take the profit before tax for the property and we divide through by the amount of equity in the property at the start of the financial year.

We calculate the equity in the property as the sum of the value of the investment property and the value of the fixtures and fittings less the outstanding mortgage balance, all at the start of the year.

In our earlier chapter on rental yield calculations, we divided through by the amount of cash we were going to invest in the deal. That makes sense as a calculation before we actually do the deal. However, now that we own the property, the better measure is to look at how the profit we have generated compares with the equity we still have invested in the property, as our equity in the property can change over time.

For Green Leaf Properties, we calculate the ROI for Property A as 7.2% (calculated as profit before tax of £2,450 ÷ equity in the property of £34,000) and we calculate the ROI for Property B to be 9.3% (profit before tax of £4,266 ÷ equity in the property of £46,000).

(iv) Capital growth (CG)

The other important component of our overall return from property is the capital growth. We calculate our investment return from capital growth as follows:

$$Capital\ growth\ (CG) = \frac{Increase\ in\ property\ value}{Equity\ in\ property}$$

That is, we take the capital growth achieved over the year and divide this through by the equity in the property at the start of the year. As noted earlier, we calculate the capital growth or increase in property value over the year as the value of the property at the end of the year less the value of the property at the start of the year.

For Green Leaf Properties, we calculate the capital growth for Property A as 14.7% (the increase in property value of £5,000 ÷ equity in the property of £34,000). The capital growth for Property B was nil this year, as the property didn't increase in value.

(v) Total return (TR)

For our final metric, we calculate the overall return achieved by each property through the ROI and capital growth combined. This metric is called total return (TR) and we calculate this as follows:

$$Total\ return\ (TR) = \frac{(Profit\ before\ tax\ + Increase\ in\ value)}{Equity\ in\ property}$$

which rearranges to

$$= \frac{Profit\ before\ tax}{Equity\ in\ property} + \frac{Increase\ in\ property\ value}{Equity\ in\ property}$$

giving

$$Total\ return\ (TR) = ROI + Capital\ growth\ (CG)$$

or

$$TR = ROI + CG$$

That is, the total return achieved by a property over the year is simply the sum of the return on investment (or ROI) and the return achieved via capital growth (or CG). What it tells us is how the total return achieved over the year, including both the profit from our property rental business and the increase in the value of the property, compare with the amount of equity we have invested.

For Green Leaf Properties, we calculate total return for Property A as 21.9% (the sum of the ROI of 7.2% and the capital growth of 14.7%). The total return for Property B this year was 9.3% (the sum of the ROI of 9.3% and the capital growth of nil).

How to calculate a multi-year average

So far, we've looked at how to calculate property returns at the total portfolio level and for our individual properties. However, we've only looked at how to calculate property returns over a single year. In practice, we will need to look at how to calculate property returns over a period of several years to truly understand the performance.

That's where calculating an average investment return over several years comes in useful.

Suppose, for example, that the total return achieved on Property A was 21.9% in Year 1, 6.5% in Year 2, and 7.0% in Year 3. How do we calculate the average return achieved? In order to do this, we need to calculate what's known in the investment industry as the *time weighted rate of return* (or TWRR). The TWRR is a measure of the compound rate of return achieved. It breaks up the return achieved into separate intervals and calculates the geometric mean of all these returns. We calculate TWRR as follows.

$$TWRR = [\,(1 + R_1) \times (1 + R_2) \times \cdots \times (1 + R_n)\,]^{1/n} - 1$$

Where R_1 is the return achieved in year 1, R_2 is the return achieved in year 2, and R_n is the return achieved in year n. As such, this formula can be extended to cover as many periods as needed. In the general formula above, this is over n time periods.

Finishing off our example

For our simple example above, we have the following inputs to the equation: R_1 = 21.9%, R_2 = 6.5%, R_3 = 7.0%, and n = 3. We calculate the average return achieved over three years as follows:

$$TWRR = [(1 + 21.9\%) \times (1 + 6.5\%) \times (1 + 7.0\%)]^{1/3} - 1 = 11.6\%$$

That is, the average total return achieved on Property A over this three-year period is 11.6% p.a. We can compare this with the average total return achieved on Property B over the same period to work out which property has performed the best.

How to use the TWRR

We can use the time weighted rate of return (TWRR) to calculate multi-year average returns for any of the metrics considered in this chapter. For example, at the property-by-property level, we could use the TWRR formula to calculate an average for the gross yield, cap rate, return on investment, capital growth or total return. At the total portfolio level, we can use the TWRR technique to calculate an average return on capital employed (ROCE) or an average return on equity (ROE) across any time period of interest to us. It's really up to you how you use it and for which performance metrics.

Finally, it's worth a quick comment on the length of the averaging period itself. To tease out the true underlying performance, you'll want to pick an averaging period long enough to average out any year-on-year fluctuations, but short enough to still be meaningful. I would recommend looking at multi-year average return metrics over the last three-year and five-year periods. But again, it's completely up to you to decide what's relevant for your portfolio and for your individual properties.

In conclusion

That brings us to the end of this chapter on how to calculate property returns. I hope that you've enjoyed it and that you're keen to use some of these techniques at your next financial year end to quantify the returns you've achieved. I would recommend preparing this type of analysis once a year as part of an annual portfolio review to better understand the returns you're achieving on your investments.

The metrics we've covered here can help us measure our property returns, understand which properties are performing the best, and tell us how the actual performance compares with the expected performance before we bought the property. They don't, however, show us why we're generating these results or what's going wrong when our returns turn out lower than we expected. Perhaps even more crucially, they don't tell us what we can do to improve the performance of our portfolio and what levers we can pull to improve our future returns.

In our next chapter, we'll dive even deeper into this topic by looking at a range of property management KPIs. These KPIs or key performance indicators will give us even greater insights into our performance and show us how we can improve returns.

Chapter 8

Property management KPIs

What gets measured, gets managed.

–Peter Drucker, *The Practice of Management*

This next chapter is all about sweating your property assets. We're going to look at how you can measure and improve performance at a slightly more granular level. In our last chapter, we introduced a range of return metrics that you can use to track performance. The techniques we introduce in this chapter will supplement these metrics and will help you to understand why your portfolio is performing the way it is. We'll also discuss what you can do to improve things.

Whether you are an experienced investor or a new investor looking to make their mark, I'm confident you will find something in here to improve what you are doing each and every day.

What are key performance indicators?

Whether it's a personal weight-loss target, a corporate target around hours worked, or an author tracking their number of words written, the goals and targets we set ourselves have the power to motivate us. Perhaps even more importantly, tracking our performance against these goals and targets forces us to face up to the reality of a situation and to be realistic about what we've achieved and where we need to focus our efforts.

In business, key performance indicators or KPIs are quantifiable metrics used to gauge performance. Businesses use KPIs to evaluate how successful they've been in a particular activity. KPIs can be set around financial or operational goals, e.g. revenue or profit. They can also be more anecdotal in nature, e.g. in-store traffic, employee retention, or perhaps customer satisfaction.

To choose the right KPIs, we need to have a good understanding of a business and what's important for its success. In this chapter, we'll look at the property management KPIs you can use for a typical property rental business. We'll look at both financial and non-financial metrics and for each of our KPIs, we'll also consider what actions we can take to improve performance.

It isn't just large real estate investment companies and investors with larger property portfolios that can benefit from developing and monitoring performance against a set of KPIs. Even investors with just one or two properties in their portfolio can use these metrics to track and improve performance.

Financial KPIs – Understanding your income

To start with, we're going to look at some important financial KPIs you can use to better understand the income side of your P&L.

In the table on the following page, I've set out some figures for one of the two properties owned by our fictitious business, Green Leaf Properties. The figures presented are for the one-bedroom apartment in Manchester that we called Property A in our last chapter. Below, I'm going to teach you how to calculate each of the metrics shown in the table, what they mean, and how you can turn them into a KPI for your property rental business.

Market rental income

The market rental income is simply the maximum amount of rent the property could theoretically collect. In an ideal world, you would charge 100% of the market rent for the property all of the time. However, this doesn't always happen in practice for a variety of reasons. Knowing the market rental income will help us understand how close our rents are to current market rents.

Income metrics and property management KPIs

Property A		£	KPI
Market rental income		9,900	
Loss to lease	(a)	(300)	3.0%
Loss to voids	(b)	(800)	8.1%
Other losses (e.g. unpaid rent)	(c)	(0)	0.0%
Actual rental income		8,800	
Other income	(d)	200	2.0%
Total revenue		9,000	

To estimate the market rental income, we need to conduct a market survey. This is a simple process and you should do this at least annually, preferably more frequently. You can do a search on Rightmove or your favourite portal to see what similar properties are being marketed for right now. The closer the comparables, the better the estimate. You can also "shop" your properties by calling some local letting agents to ask them what the property could let for in the current market. Call as both a landlord and a tenant and see if the answers differ. To avoid overly optimistic estimates, ask the agent what rent you would need to market the property at to guarantee (with 100% certainty) that you could let the property out within two weeks or four weeks of it coming on to the market.

For Greenleaf Properties, our market research revealed that the current market rent for a large one-bedroom apartment of this size is around £825 pcm. To calculate the market rental income, we multiply this by 12 to get an annual figure of £9,900.

(a) Loss to lease

Loss to lease can be a little tricky to explain and some people find it confusing the first time they encounter it. I'll try to keep it as simple as I can. Loss to lease is the difference between the market rental income and the potential rental income at the current agreed rent. It assumes that the property is 100% occupied all year round with no voids and no missed payments.

$$Loss\ to\ lease = Market\ rental\ income - Potential\ rental\ income$$

Let's look at a simple example. We calculated the market rental income above at £9,900. We then calculate the potential rental income based on the agreed level of rent. This property is currently let out for £800 pcm, so we calculate the potential rental income by multiplying £800 pcm by 12 to get £9,600. From this, we can see that the potential rental income is the rental income we would have achieved if the property were 100% occupied all year round at the agreed rent. Finally, we calculate the loss to lease as the difference between these figures, i.e. £9,900 – £9,600 which equals £300.

In the table on the previous page, I have shown the loss to lease as a negative number. This is because the £300 is the loss to our rental income that's caused by renting out the apartment for £25 pcm less than the market rent. A zero loss to lease, therefore, tells us that our rent is set in line with the market rent. And a large loss to lease tells us that a property is let below the market rent.

Using loss to lease as a KPI

We can turn loss to lease into a KPI by expressing the loss to lease as a percentage of the market rental income. That is, we can calculate the following metric, which I've presented on the far-right column of the table above.

$$Loss\ to\ lease\ \% = \frac{Loss\ to\ lease}{Market\ rental\ income}$$

Expressed as a percentage, this KPI tells us what percentage of the maximum theoretical rental income from this property we have lost by setting our actual rents below the market rent.

For Green Leaf Properties, the loss to lease % is calculated as (£9,900 – £9,600) ÷ £9,900 which equals 3.0%. So, we've lost 3.0% of the market rental income from a below market rent.

More on loss to lease

Lots of new property investors ask why there is a difference between market rental income and potential rental income. There are many reasons why this might be the case. One possible reason is that the landlord has not reviewed the rent and so the rent has not been increased in a while. Another potential reason is that the landlord has reviewed the rent and was aware of the higher market rent. However, they have chosen not to increase the rent in order to encourage a tenant to stay longer.

It's important to stress here that I'm not suggesting the rent should be set exactly in line with the market rent 100% of the time. However, I am saying that you should aim to agree rents which are more or less in line with current market rents, within a certain degree of tolerance. Otherwise, you are losing out on potential income.

One of the biggest costs in a property rental business is the cost of "turning over" a property at the end of a tenancy. As we've mentioned before, in between tenancies you'll likely incur additional cleaning, marketing and utility costs. As such, it's a perfectly valid strategy to leave the current level of rent unchanged to encourage a tenant to stay longer. However, there comes a point where the loss to lease from not increasing the rent is actually greater than the additional costs incurred in turning over the property.

How to improve loss to lease

Each investor will have their own tolerance levels here. But to give you some guidance, I try to make sure that my rents are set within 5% of the market rent. For Green Leaf Properties, the rent for Property A is within 3% of the market rent, so this would be acceptable from my perspective. My loss to lease target, therefore, is that this KPI is less than or equal to 5% across my portfolio as a whole.

Improving loss to lease is fairly straightforward. You should review the market rents regularly to make sure they are tracking the local market. At the end of a tenancy, you should speak to your letting agent about what level of rent you can hope to achieve. If you manage the property yourself, you can shop the property or review the portals to get a feeling for current market rents.

A longer list of ideas

There are also a number of practical things you can do to make sure your property is viewed at its best. This will give you the best chance to secure top dollar for the property. Here are just a few ideas.

- Advertise early – Advertise before the end of the existing tenancy comes to an end to increase the number of leads generated
- Cleaning – Get the property cleaned on day one of the void period to ensure the property is viewed at its best
- Take great photos and run a great advert – You want to attract a lot of attention and drum up multiple interested parties
- Negotiate – For example, if a new tenant wants extra storage, you could agree to provide this if they agree to pay full asking rent
- Viewings – Consider the time of day the property looks at its best, open the curtains, and make sure it smells nice
- Start date – Being flexible on dates can help you secure a good rent, but a long void period will likely cost you more
- Furnishings – Ensure any furniture provided is good quality

If you are going to use a letting agent, make sure they are doing all these things on your behalf. At my last turn around, after the cleaning was complete, we asked the letting agent to buy a couple of brand-new mattress protectors and leave them on the beds sealed to give the property a 'new to market' feel. This is a bit like when a hotel covers that glass in your room with plastic wrap. They do this to signal that no-one has used it before. Little touches like this can give your property a more up-market feel.

(b) Loss to voids

The loss to voids is fairly straightforward. This is the amount of rental income lost this year when the property was sitting empty. For Green Leaf Properties, the one-bedroom apartment was sat empty for one whole month in between tenancies. As such, the loss to voids was a whole month's rent of £800. Again, this is shown as a negative in the table, as it's a loss versus the market rental income.

More generally, loss to voids can be calculated using the following formula based on the number of days the property was vacant.

$$Loss\ to\ voids = \left(\frac{Number\ of\ void\ days}{365\ days}\right) \times potential\ rental\ income$$

We should aim to keep the loss to voids as small as possible by turning around each property quickly. Between tenancies, we are still incurring expenses, e.g. mortgage costs, as well. Certain of these costs, e.g. like council tax and utility bills, will only be incurred during voids.

Using loss to voids as a KPI

We can turn loss to voids into a KPI by expressing the loss to voids as a percentage of the market rental income. That is, we can calculate the following metric, again shown on the far-right column of the table presented previously.

$$Loss\ to\ voids\ \% = \frac{Loss\ to\ voids}{Market\ rental\ income}$$

This KPI tells us what percentage of the maximum rental income we have lost from voids. For Green Leaf Properties, the loss to voids % is calculated as £800 ÷ £9,900 which equals 8.1%. So, we've lost 8.1% of our market rental income from the one-month void period.

Every investor will have their own tolerance level. Generally, I aim to keep the loss to voids below 5% when averaged over several years. In practice, this means that I need to keep voids to less than two weeks if my tenant changes every year. If my tenant stays for two years, I will have more like a month or so to turn around the property.

How to improve loss to voids

There are two general strategies you can employ to reduce the loss to voids. The first strategy is to encourage the tenant to stay for longer. A competitively priced rent will help with this, as will taking care of existing tenants and responding to their requests promptly. Letting a property unfurnished can also help, as the effort put into furnishing a property creates a barrier to them leaving.

We will come back to the question of how to measure and improve tenant satisfaction later in this chapter, so I won't say anymore on this topic for now.

The second strategy is to do everything you can to turn the property around quickly. The single biggest thing you can do here is get your agent to start marketing the property a month or two before the existing tenancy ends and to line up some viewings in advance. You should also make sure you attend to any cleaning required or repairs needed as soon as possible after the tenant leaves.

Finally, you could even consider offering some kind of incentive or reward to encourage the tenant to stay for longer. I've heard of landlords and investors providing a move-in hamper and sending their tenant Christmas cards. I've even heard stories of landlords offering to kit an apartment out with a state-of-the-art, flat-screen TV if the tenant stays for five years or more. Remember that most tenants are buying a lifestyle, not just a roof over their head. Use this to your advantage and give them a compelling reason to stay.

(c) Other losses

There are a number of things that go into the 'other losses' line. The main one is rental arrears, i.e. rental income that was due but that the tenant never paid. In addition, you could also include losses incurred where the tenancy deposit was insufficient to cover any damage left by the tenant.

For Green Leaf Properties, all the rental income due in the year was paid and there were no damage-related costs at the end of the tenancy. The other losses are shown as zero.

Using other losses as a KPI

We can turn other losses into a KPI by expressing these losses as a percentage of the market rental income. That is, we can calculate the following metric, shown on the far-right column of the table.

$$Other\ losses\ \% = \frac{Other\ losses}{Market\ rental\ income}$$

This KPI tells us what percentage of the maximum rental income we lost from other losses. For Green Leaf Properties, the other losses % is calculated as £0 ÷ £9,900 which equals 0%. That is, we've lost none of our market rental income from other losses.

In general, I aim to keep the other losses % as nil for my properties, although the level of rental arrears and damage will vary from property to property. I try to invest in strong city centre locations and choose professional tenants, so I aim for a very low other losses %. Depending on the location of your properties and the demographic profile of tenants in those areas, you might find that you do need to budget for some level of other losses.

How to improve other losses?

Improving the other losses metric is all about your choice of property and your choice of tenant. If you invest in high-quality properties in nice locations and if you vet tenants carefully, you should experience a relatively low level of rental arrears and losses related to damage. Make sure you screen tenants carefully through your reference checks and absolutely do not give someone the benefit of the doubt. If they have bad credit history, you should insist on a guarantor or better still look for another tenant.

Where I can, I try to stick to tenants with a strong employment history. By this, I mean that I look for both long service with a single employer and some level of professional qualifications in an industry that is going to be in demand for some time. No industry is 100% recession-proof and you never truly know a tenant until they move in. However, you can certainly try your best to avoid problem tenants.

Actual rental income

The actual rental income is simply the actual amount of rent you've collected on this property over the year. It's equal to the market rental income minus the loss to lease, the loss to voids and the other losses.

For Greenleaf Properties, our actual rental income this year is the market rental income of £9,900 minus £300 for the loss to lease and £800 for the loss to voids. This gives us an actual rental income of £8,800 for this financial year.

Calculating the economic vacancy

Finally, we're going to wrap this discussion up by looking at a metric which combines these three KPIs in to a single number. This metric is known as the *economic vacancy* and it's calculated as follows.

$$Economic\ vacancy\ = \frac{Loss\ to\ lease + Loss\ to\ voids + Other\ losses}{Market\ rental\ income}$$

which is equal to the following

$$= Loss\ to\ lease\ \% + Loss\ to\ voids\ \% + Other\ losses\ \%$$

The economic vacancy then tells us what percentage of the maximum rental income we have lost from a combination of below market rent, void periods and rental arrears. For Green Leaf Properties, the economic vacancy for this property is therefore the loss to lease of 3.0% plus the loss to voids of 8.1% which equals 11.1%. To get this figure down, we'll need to think about how to reduce our voids.

In addition to setting targets for loss to lease, loss to voids and other losses individually, it's good to set an overall economic vacancy target. I try to keep the economic vacancy to less than 10% for each of the properties in my portfolio.

(d) Other income

It is possible for you to make extra income from your investments in addition to rental income. We've captured this extra income in the other income metric at the bottom of the table. This area doesn't often get attention in property investment books, but if you can generate some extra income, it has the ability to turn an average property investment into a great one.

The types of extra income you can generate will depend on what's common in the local market, your management philosophy, and the type of business you want to run. You'll also be constrained by any local laws and regulations around fees that you can and can't charge your tenants. The important thing is to think about this more as a business opportunity.

For Green Leaf Properties, we've generated £200 of other income over the year by offering a monthly cleaning service. To express this as a KPI, we simply divide this amount through by the market rental income. That is, £200 ÷ £9,900 equals 2.0%. This tells us how much other income we've managed to generate, expressed as a percentage of market rent.

Some ideas for extra income generation

Here's a quick list of ideas and some areas where you might be able to generate extra income from your investments.

- Parking – Depending on supply and demand in the local area, you could charge anywhere from £50 to £150 per month for parking. On the supply side, you could buy a space yourself or you could rent one from someone else.

- Monthly pet rent – Pet owners often have a more limited choice of accommodation, as lots of landlords will not accept pets of any kind. As such, pet owners will pay more rent. You could charge £25 to £50 a month, depending on the pet.

- Cleaning service – You could write to tenants and offer them a cleaning service for a fixed fee each week or month and then arrange for this to be provided by a local cleaner. If the fee you charge the tenant is greater than the cost of hiring a cleaner to provide this service, then you're in the money.

- Laundry service – You could offer a laundry service for a fee, perhaps a pick up and return dry cleaning service. Again, you could charge a fee, then cut a deal with a local dry cleaner.

- Moving in and out – There might be opportunities for renting out storage space or supporting tenants in the move.

- Buy-out fees – You could perhaps, subject to the tenant fees ban, charge one month's rent for lease breaks.

These are just a few ideas, but I'm sure there are many more you could use to generate extra income. I've heard stories of people charging for furniture hire and adding additional rent to cover the cost of utilities. I've even heard of someone running a bike rental service as part of their business.

There are lots of opportunities in this space for creative investors. You never know, you might even end up starting a side business in the process.

Total revenue

Lastly, the final line in the table is the total revenue line. This is simply the sum of the actual rental income and any other income we've managed to generate from the property. For Green Leaf Properties, the total revenue generated from Property A is the actual rental income of £8,800 plus other income of £200 which equals £9,000. This ties up with our P&L account for Property A.

That's the income side taken care of. Now let's take a look at some property management KPIs relating to your property expenses.

Financial KPIs – Understanding your expenses

In general, running costs are much more controllable than income. For this reason, controlling expenses is the single most important thing you can do to improve the profitability of your portfolio. You should pay close attention to your budgeted expenses throughout the year to make sure these are on-track. If they go off-track, you should look into why this has happened.

In the table on the following page, I've set out figures relating to Property A, our one-bedroom apartment in Manchester. We're going to look at each expense line in turn and think about what expenses are included and how you can reduce these.

(a) Ground rent and service cost

If you own an apartment or a leasehold house, then you will likely be incurring expenses in relation to ground rent and service costs. The level of ground rent will be specified in the terms of the lease agreement. And the service cost will be calculated and billed each year by the management company, based on the cost of the works carried out over the year.

Expense metrics and property management KPIs

Property A		£	KPI
Ground rent and service cost	(a)	1,300	
Legal and professional fees	(b)	1,080	12.2%
Premises insurance	(c)	420	
Cost of services provided	(d)	218	
Property repairs and maintenance	(e)	60	0.7%
Cost of sales		3,078	
Finance costs	(f)	3,072	3.3%
Total expenses		6,150	

For Green Leaf Properties, the ground rent incurred over the year was £250 and the service charges were £1,050 in total.

For the most part, there's very little you can do to try to control these costs. If the building has a residents' committee involved in the appointment and scrutiny of the management company, you could get involved in this to try to help control costs. However, there's likely to be a big time commitment for a limited reward here. For me, it's all about due diligence in the deal assessment phase. If you've budgeted correctly in your cash flows and modelling, then hopefully there are no surprises for you here.

There's no need for a KPI to track this performance, as these costs are largely out of our control.

(b) Legal and professional fees

If you use a letting agent to manage your property for you, the bulk of these expenses will be property management fees. It will also include any costs in relation to the marketing of the property in between tenancies and any tenancy renewal costs.

For Green Leaf properties, the total cost of £1,080 breaks down as follows: £880 for property management, that is, 10% of the £8,800 collected in rent; £200 for the marketing of the property in between tenancies.

The property management fee is likely charged as a percentage of the rent collected from the property. As such, it makes sense for us to turn this into a KPI by expressing the legal and professional fees charged over the year as a percentage of the actual rental income from the property as follows.

$$Professional\ fees\ \% = \frac{Legal\ and\ professional\ fees}{Actual\ rental\ income}$$

For Green Leaf Properties, we have calculated this in the right-hand column of the table as £1,080 ÷ £8,800 equals 12.3%. That is, we've paid out 12.3% of the actual rental income collected in legal and professional fees over the year.

To improve this KPI, you can shop around for the best deal on property management fees with agents in the local area. It's not all about fees though, it's about quality of service too. And if the service you're getting is good, you might be happy to pay a little more.

As your portfolio grows, you might be able to use its larger size and the greater income potential for the letting agent to cut yourself a better deal on fees. Alternatively, you could consider managing the properties yourself to reduce fees.

(c) Premises insurance

This category of expenses will include things like buildings insurance and landlord's insurance. The latter provides protection against property damage and public liability insurance. If you own a house, you will likely be arranging the buildings cover yourself. If you own an apartment, this will likely be arranged for the block as a whole by the property management company.

For these expenses, there are only a few things that you can do to impact the amount you will need to pay. For the policies you arrange yourself, you can call an insurance broker and get competing bids to try to lower the cost. You might also be able to play around with the level of cover and the excesses on the policy. However, do make sure that the policy still meets your needs.

For Green Leaf Properties, the total cost of £420 is in relation to buildings insurance cover costing £360 and a separate policy for public liability insurance costing £60 for the year.

The other category of insurance that we haven't covered here is rent guarantee insurance. This type of policy pays out if a tenant stops paying rent. In general, I try to insure only those risks which would result in a large loss. So, I don't typically take out this type of policy. In my view, it's better to manage this risk through proper screening of tenants. Also, as your portfolio grows in size, the risks around non-payment reduce as a result of diversification. That is, with a large portfolio, the likelihood of all tenants defaulting on their rent at the same time is low, absent some big economic shock. More on this in the next chapter.

(d) Cost of services provided

This line typically includes things like the cost of utilities, e.g. council tax, electricity and water, in the void period. Also, if you provide any additional services to your tenant, then the cost of providing these should be included here.

For Green Leaf Properties, the cost of services provided is £218. This cost breaks down as £100 for one month's council tax and £18 for electricity costs in the void period. In addition, the cost of hiring a cleaner to provide the monthly cleaning service was £100.

The levers you can pull to reduce these costs will depend on the property involved and the types of cost incurred. Things like utility bills for void periods can be reduced by making sure there are no appliances running while the property is empty. The cost of any time-related expenses like council tax can be minimised by reducing the length of the void period.

(e) Property repairs and maintenance

These costs will vary depending on the age, type and state of repair of the property. They will also vary with the speed at which you or your letting agent reacts to any maintenance requests. Costs that fall into this category include painting and decorating, electrical repairs, heating and plumbing repairs, gas and electrical safety checks, and pest control.

For Green Leaf Properties, it was an excellent year from a repairs and maintenance perspective. The costs in this category were limited to £60 only for a gas safety check. It's good to track and average these costs over a number of years as they can fluctuate.

We can turn this expense category into a KPI by expressing the total repairs and maintenance cost as a percentage of the actual rental income from the property:

$$Repairs\ and\ maintenance\ \% = \frac{Cost\ of\ repairs\ and\ maintenance}{Actual\ rental\ income}$$

For Green Leaf Properties, we have calculated this in the right-hand column of the table as £60 ÷ £8,800 equals 0.7%. That is, we've paid out 0.7% of the actual rental income in repairs and maintenance costs over the year.

Actions you can take to reduce these costs include shopping around for tradespeople if you're managing the property yourself. Also, you should make sure you act on any repair and maintenance requests promptly to prevent further damage. As the old saying goes, a stitch in time saves nine. If you are using a letting agent, then make sure they are managing tradespeople well and responding quickly to any repair requests.

(f) Finance costs

Finally, we come to our biggest property expense, finance costs. This category includes the interest expense on any loans or mortgages used to purchase a property. It also includes any one-off costs associated with re-mortgaging a property. We can turn this expense category into a KPI by expressing the finance costs as a percentage of the outstanding mortgage balance as follows.

$$Finance\ costs\ \% = \frac{Finance\ costs}{Mortgage\ balance}$$

For Green Leaf Properties, the finance costs incurred over the year were £3,072. These costs were 100% related to the interest expense incurred on the mortgage associated with this property. To calculate the KPI, we take the £3,072 and divide by the outstanding mortgage balance of £93,000 to get 3.3%. That is, we're paying an interest rate of 3.3% p.a. on these borrowings.

The main lever we can pull to improve this KPI is to shop around for a better mortgage deal. At the end of each fixed-rate period, speak to your mortgage broker to see whether there are better mortgage deals on the market. This is likely going to be your biggest expense, so shopping around for a good deal here is well worth the time and effort. You could also consider using any profits you generate to pay down your mortgage balances.

Some non-financial KPIs

So far, our discussion has been limited to financial KPIs. However, depending on the aims and objectives of your business, you can also set some non-financial KPIs for your portfolio.

These KPIs can be operational in nature to make sure that you are meeting the minimum legal standards. Or they can be supporting metrics that will help you meet the other financial targets that you have set. A good example is tenant satisfaction. A high level of tenant satisfaction means tenants will likely stay for longer. This in turn will help you achieve a lower loss to voids % and will help you to improve your investment returns. In the list below, I've suggested some areas where you could consider setting some non-financial KPIs.

Tenant satisfaction

- Tenant satisfaction – You could design a tenant satisfaction survey, e.g. using SurveyMonkey, and monitor these tenant satisfaction scores over time.

- Time to complete repairs – One of the biggest frustrations for tenants is landlords who don't respond quickly. Why not set yourself a KPI around the number of days taken to respond to requests and complete repairs.

- Suggestions box – Write out to your tenants and ask for their suggestions and about any niggles or frustrations they have.

Legal and regulatory

- New tenancy set up – You can set yourself KPIs around having tenancy agreements in place, deposits registered, the correct documents issued at the start of each tenancy to help you meet the minimum legal requirements.

- Safety testing – You'll need to make sure all the safety testing requirements for your properties are carried out in a timely manner. This will include things like gas and electrical safety checks. Set yourself some KPIs around these.

Environmental impact

- EPC rating – There is evidence that eco-friendly properties with lower environmental impacts attract higher capital growth and rental income. Set a minimum EPC rating for your properties and use this as a KPI over time.

Tenant quality

- Inspections – Use inspections to understand how well tenants are looking after your properties. Set yourself some KPIs, e.g. that all tenants are achieving a minimum inspection rating of 'satisfactory' with no major damage.

- Incidents of damage – Monitor the number of incidents of damage and set yourself a KPI around this. If there are too many incidents, you will need to figure out why and what you can do about this.

These are just some of the suggestions I've come up with for non-financial KPIs you might like to monitor. Now that you know all about key performance indicators, feel free to add you own and set yourself some ambitious targets.

In conclusion

Monitoring performance using a range of property management KPIs is the best way to understand your returns. If your investments are not working out as expected, then the KPIs we've discussed here will help you work out why and what you can do about it.

I cannot stress how important this type of analysis is for achieving top level performance. Studying your portfolio at the property-by-property level and breaking down all the factors that contribute to that performance can be extremely enlightening. Moreover, setting targets for the various property management KPIs will force you to be objective about the results your achieving, act as a catalyst for any action that's needed, and keep you focussed over the long term.

Chapter 9

Portfolio risk management

It ain't what you don't know that gets you into trouble. It's what you know for sure that just ain't so.

–Mark Twain

Our penultimate chapter is one on portfolio risk management for property investors. We're going to look at the types of risk inherent in running a buy-to-let property rental business and what you can do to manage these risks better. Good risk management can help you survive a property crash and weather an economic storm, so it's important and not to be overlooked.

An introduction to risk management

Running a property rental business exposes an investor to all kinds of risk. There are property-specific risks, such as tenants defaulting on their rental payments or causing damage to your property. There are also external risks, like changes in market rents or interest rates. And how you manage these risks over the long term will impact on the success of your investments.

Risk management is the process of identifying, quantifying and controlling these risks. The theory goes that by establishing a good risk management plan, which considers potential risks before they occur, a business can take steps to protect its profitability and safeguard its future. Risk management plans can help businesses to avoid potential threats and minimise the impact if they do occur. They can also help businesses take advantage of any potential upsides.

There's a vast amount of literature out there on *enterprise risk management* (or ERM). Lots of this is quite esoteric and not particularly helpful to the average investor. So, I'm going to ignore all the formal frameworks and technical language and look at this topic from a more intuitive standpoint. However, I will make use of some simple formulae and probability models to help quantify the impact of certain risks. These models will also help us in planning our risk response.

In the first part of the chapter, we're going to run through the five most important risks you'll need to manage as a property investor. In the second part, we'll take a brief look at some other risks you should think about and briefly discuss the idea of "resilience testing" your portfolio.

The top five risks for property investors

For each risk, I'm going to provide a definition, look at how you can quantify the impact and discuss what actions you can take to mitigate or transfer the risk.

(1) Liquidity risk

Liquidity risk is the risk that a business cannot meet its short-term obligations. That is, it's the risk that the business runs out of cash and cannot pay those people or businesses that it owes money too.

For a property rental business, the principal risk is that your investment portfolio turns cash flow negative and you don't have a sufficient amount of liquid assets set aside to cover the cash outflow. Individual properties can turn cash flow negative over the short or medium term for a variety of reasons.

- a tenant defaults and stops paying their rent
- an unexpected large repair, e.g. a boiler replacement
- an extended void period, possibly with expenses

I've talked about the actions you can take to minimise voids in our previous chapter, so I won't cover that again here.

A reserve fund for repairs

When it comes to the risk of unexpected large repairs, there's no way to insure this risk. As property investors, our only option is to hold a cash reserve to cover such expenses. The question we're left with is how to quantify this risk and how much of a reserve we need.

In general, I try not to overcomplicate this. It's clear that as the size of our property portfolio increases, we're going to need a bigger reserve – we own more properties, so more things can go wrong. The cost of a large, one-off repair in a single property could be of the order of £2,000 or so. And, in any given year, we'd be very unlucky if more than half of our properties needed a repair like this. As such, I simply set aside £2,000 for half of my properties as a reserve fund for repairs. So, if I had five properties in my investment portfolio, I would set aside 5 × £2,000 ÷ 2 = £5,000 to cover any large repair costs. If I had to dip into this reserve fund over the course of the year, I'd try to top it up again straight afterwards from rental profits.

A reserve fund for tenant defaults

For tenant default risk, you could look for an insurance solution. For example, you could take out a rent guarantee policy which pays the rent when a tenant defaults. The expense associated with this type of cover does reduce your cash flow and your investment returns, so I'm going to assume here that we decide not to take this cover. In that case, we'll need to set aside a cash reserve to cover our normal property expenses in the case that a tenant defaults.

When it comes to quantifying the size of this cash reserve, I like to get a bit more scientific. It's clear that as the size of my portfolio increases, the default risk reduces to some extent. For example, if I own one property, it's a real possibility that this tenant could default – in effect, 100% of my portfolio has defaulted. However, if I own ten properties, then it's extremely unlikely all ten of my tenants would default at the same time. This is the benefit of diversification.

But is there something we can do to quantify how much of a benefit we get from this kind of diversification and can we turn this into a rule of thumb around how much of a cash reserve we need to hold? The answer to this is yes.

A model for tenant defaults

Suppose we want to hold in our reserve fund enough cash to cover the next year's expenses for all properties where there is a default in the year. We're going to assume that if a tenant defaults, they default at the start of the year. In practice, it can take up to twelve months to evict a tenant in default, so this is not an unreasonable assumption. Also, we'll assume that for each property the average expenses are around £6,000 per year. This is close to the average annual expense outgo for Property A and Property B in our Green Leaf Properties example, once we've stripped out the management fees.

As a rule, we're going to set the size of the reserve fund equal to the amount we'd need to be 99% certain we will have enough cash in the next twelve months. This is a prudent estimate (i.e. there's only a 1% chance we won't have enough cash) based on a probability model that I'll describe in just a moment. Finally, we're going to assume that the risk of a single tenant defaulting in any given year is 10% or 0.1. This is the average tenant default rate for the private rented sector in the UK based on historical data. This also means that the probably of a tenant not defaulting in any given year is 90% or 0.9. Right, time for some examples.

The one property case

The table below shows the potential outcomes if we have just one property in our portfolio. There are two potential outcomes. The first is that for Property 1 there is no default, which we've labelled as *ND*; the second is that for Property 1 there is a default, which we've labelled as *D*. The probabilities associated with these outcomes are shown in the last column. They sum to 1.

Default model – Outcomes and probabilities for one property case

Outcome	Property 1	No. defaults, N	Probability
1	*ND*	0	0.9
2	*D*	1	0.1
Total			1.0

If I hold a cash reserve of nil, this will be sufficient in the case where there are no defaults, i.e. for Outcome 1. However, it won't be enough to cover our expenses when there's one default, i.e. for Outcome 2. There's still a 10% chance of Outcome 2 happening, which is greater than the criteria we set ourselves above, i.e. that there needs to be a 99% chance we won't run out of cash.

Based on this logic, we need to hold £6,000 in our reserve fund to cover tenant defaults. If we did this, we'd have enough to cover the expenses for both the zero defaults case and the one default case. And the probability of achieving one of these two outcomes is 100%, i.e. we're 100% certain to have enough cash. This meets the criteria we set ourselves. Still with me? Let's move on to two properties.

The two property case

The table below shows the potential outcomes if we have two properties in our portfolio. There are four potential outcomes now. The first is that there is no default for either property. The second is that Property One defaults and Property 2 does not default. The third is that Property One doesn't default, but Property Two does default. The last is that both properties default.

The probabilities associated with these outcomes are calculated in the last column. For example, the probability that neither property defaults is 0.9 (Property 1 doesn't default) × 0.9 (Property 2 doesn't default) = 0.81. So, there is an 81% chance that we get Outcome 1, where neither property defaults. Again, the sum of the probabilities over these four outcomes is equal to 1.

Default model – Outcomes and probabilities for two property case

Outcome	Property 1	Property 2	No. defaults, N	Probability
1	ND	ND	0	0.9 × 0.9 = 0.81
2	D	ND	1	0.1 × 0.9 = 0.09
3	ND	D	1	0.9 × 0.1 = 0.09
4	D	D	2	0.1 × 0.1 = 0.01
Total				1.00

Again, let's look at the size of the reserve fund we'd need based on the rule we made at the start of this section. If we held £12,000, i.e. two lots of £6,000, then we'd have enough to cover two defaults. That is, we'd have enough of a reserve fund to be 100% certain we could meet our expenses.

Can we get away with less?

Well, if we held £6,000, enough to cover the expenses for just one default, then this would be sufficient to cover the expenses for delinquent properties under Outcomes 1, 2 and 3 set out in the table above. For each of Outcomes 1, 2 and 3, the number of properties in default is 1 or less – that is, N in the fourth column of the table is less than or equal to 1 for each of these three outcomes. And the combined probability that we get one of these three outcomes is $0.81 + 0.09 + 0.09 = 0.99$. That is, we are 99% certain that we'll get one of these three outcomes. So, we can be 99% certain that by holding just £6,000, we won't run out of cash over the year.

The above shows us the benefit of diversification. That is, we need to hold £6,000 in both the one property case and the two property case to be 99% certain that we have enough cash in our reserve fund to cover the expenses for properties in default. That is, our reserve fund didn't need to increase as the size of our portfolio grew from one property to two properties.

Extending this model

In order to generalise this to more properties, let's rejig the table we used above for the two property case into the following format.

Default model – Cumulative probabilities for two property case

No. defaults, N	Probability	Cumulative Probability
0	0.81	0.81
1	0.18	0.99
2	0.01	1.00

In this table, the left-hand column shows the number of defaults. The middle column shows the probability of getting this number of defaults. So, for $N = 0$, we take the 0.81 from our previous table. For $N = 1$, we add together the probabilities for each of the outcomes where $N = 1$. That is, 0.09 (Outcome 2) + 0.09 (Outcome 3) = 0.18 from the previous table. For $N = 2$, we simply take the 0.01.

Finally, the last column on the right shows the cumulative probability, or the running total, of the previous rows. To illustrate what I mean, the probability of getting one or fewer defaults is the sum of the probabilities for $N = 1$ and $N = 0$, i.e. 0.18 + 0.81 = 0.99. Likewise, the probability of getting two or fewer defaults is the sum of the probabilities for $N = 2$, $N = 1$, and $N = 0$, i.e. 0.01 + 0.18 + 0.99 = 1.

We can use this revised table and the cumulative probabilities in the last column to choose the 'cut-off point' for the size of our reserve fund. For example, if we want to be 99% certain we won't run out of cash, then we can look down the last column and look for the first row where the cumulative probability hits 99% or 0.99. In the table above, this is for $N = 1$. From this, we know that the probability of getting one default or less (i.e. that N equals 1 or less) is 99%. So, if we hold just one property's worth of expenses, i.e. 1 × £6,000, we can be 99% sure that we won't run out of cash.

The three property case

For the three property case, I'm going to jump straight to the table of cumulative probabilities. Feel free to list out all the possible outcomes and calculate the cumulative probabilities for yourself if you like as a check on my maths.

Default model – Cumulative probabilities for three property case

No. defaults, N	Probability	Cumulative Probability
0	0.729	0.729
1	0.243	0.972
2	0.027	0.999
3	0.001	1.000

Let's choose our cut-off point. Looking down the last column, we can see that the first cumulative probability that's over 99% or 0.99 is for the row where $N = 2$. So, if we hold two properties worth expenses, i.e. 2 × £6,000 = £12,000, we can be at least 99% certain we won't run out of cash.

You can check these probabilities using an online calculator for a binomial distribution, which is the mathematical name for the model we're using here. If you type something like "binomial distribution online calculator" into your favourite search engine, you'll find a range of these tools online. Simply input 0.1 as the 'probability of success', which here is the probability of one of our tenants defaulting. In addition, you can input the number of properties in your portfolio, which is three for the three property case above. Then, depending on the calculator you're using, you can read off the probabilities and cumulative probabilities.

Bringing it all together

We can extend the model above to calculate the size of the reserve fund we'd need for any number of properties. In the table below, I've calculated the size of the reserve fund you'd need to be 99% certain you wouldn't run out of cash, using the method we've set out above.

Default model – Reserve fund needed versus number of properties

Number of properties	Cut-off point, N=?	Reserve fund
1	1	£6,000
2	1	£6,000
3	2	£12,000
4	2	£12,000
5	2	£12,000
10	4	£24,000
15	5	£30,000
20	6	£36,000
30	7	£42,000
40	9	£54,000
50	10	£60,000

The left column shows the number of properties in the portfolio. The middle column lists the value of *N* for which we can be 99% certain that we will have this many or fewer defaults, i.e. it's the "number of properties worth" of expenses we need to hold to be 99% certain we won't run out of cash. We pick this *N* using the technique as described above for choosing the cut-off point, by reading down the cumulative probability totals and picking the first row over 99% or 0.99. The last column shows the size of the reserve fund needed.

Adapting this approach

Using this simple binomial distribution model, we've calculated how the size of the reserve fund should scale with the number of properties in our portfolio. You can see that because of diversification, the size of the reserve fund needed increases quite slowly as the number of properties increases. However, now we've been able to quantify this benefit using a simple probability.

The key assumption I've made in the analysis presented above is that the probability of default is 10% or 0.1 for the private rented sector. If you rent to social tenants, the average probability of default is more like 25% or 0.25 from historical data. So, if you rent to social tenants you'll need to re-run the analysis above using an online calculator of your choosing with the probability of default set to 0.25 instead. We've also assumed that the probability of tenants defaulting is independent of each other. This might be true in normal times, but if the UK was hit by a bad recession, the default rate may rise all across your portfolio at the same time. You could model such an event by using a higher default rate in the model above.

Finally, we've ignored the fact that even though certain properties might be in default, other properties in our portfolio will likely still be cash flow positive (hopefully). This means the estimate above is likely to be a prudent estimate of the cash reserve needed.

Final comments on liquidity risk

Bringing together the two pieces of analysis above, we could calculate how big a reserve fund we'd need to cover unexpected large repairs and tenant defaults in the next twelve months. For example, if I had five properties in my portfolio, I would hold 5 × £2,000 ÷ 2 = £5,000 to cover unexpected large repairs. From the table above, I'd also hold £12,000 to cover tenant defaults. In total, therefore, I'd be wanting to hold a cash buffer of £17,000 against these risks and make sure I have enough liquid assets if I need them.

This might sound like a large cash buffer to hold, but it's worth remembering that if things go wrong here, then your portfolio could go insolvent. When you've only got a small number of properties in your portfolio, you might be more relaxed on this point, e.g. if you feel you could add in some extra cash from elsewhere should you need it. However, as your portfolio grows in size, you'll need to be more systematic in the way that you manage this kind of liquidity risk. For a large portfolio, there's almost no chance you could add the extra cash needed if things do go wrong – the size of the problem has increased relative to your other earnings. At this level and size, you'll need to make sure your portfolio is self-sufficient. This kind of tenant default model can help here.

You can play around with all the parameters in this model to suit yourself. Change the average expenses per property, the probability of default, or even the number of years expenses you want to be able to cover. You can use the model as a stress test, e.g. to model what would happen in a bad recession if defaults rose to 30% or more in a single year. How much cash would I need then?

A final word of warning

Please do remember that what I've presented here is only one possible model you could use to set the size of a reserve fund. I'm not advocating the use of this particular model, but I am trying to give you a feel for how a bit of statistical modelling can help you in sizing up the problem. Any model is only as good as the assumptions it's based on. The assumptions you use in your own modelling should be carefully thought through and where possible based on actual data, rather than gut feel.

(2) Interest rate risk

Interest rate risk is the risk that the profitability of a business changes due to changes in interest rates in the economy. In the main, it's the risk that your borrowing costs will go up and your profits will reduce as interest rates increase.

For a property rental business, this is one of the biggest risks you will face. In general, property investors borrow a large portion of the cost of buying an investment property via mortgage financing. So, the cost of servicing that debt is typically one of the property investor's biggest expenses.

Quantifying this risk

One of the ways to gauge the size of this risk is to use a formula from the accounting world known as *interest cover*. Interest on borrowings and mortgages has to be paid before the business owners can realise any profits. So, a good measure of this risk is to compare the available operating profit with the amount of interest being paid on the debt.

$$Interest\ cover = \frac{Operating\ profit}{Finance\ costs}$$

In general, the lower the value of this ratio, the more the company is burdened by debt expenses. When a business's interest cover is only 1.5 or lower, then its ability to meet finance costs in the future may be questionable. In the formula above, I have assumed that you take out interest-only mortgages, so the only debt-servicing cost is the interest expense itself. If you use repayment mortgages, you could adapt the formula above to replace finance costs with your total mortgage repayments.

Let's look at a quick example. For Green Leaf Properties, we take our operating profit of £12,326 and divide by the finance costs of £7,164 (figures from Chapter 7). This gives an interest cover of 1.72 for the year to 31 March 2020.

Stress testing your portfolio

I like to consider how the profitability of my portfolio and the interest cover would change in the following two situations.

(a) Future refinancing

Suppose that at the end of my five-year fixed rate mortgages, the rate I'm paying will increase to around 5% p.a. If I can't refinance on to a lower rate, I'll be stuck at this 5% p.a. interest rate. I like to think of this as my *refinancing risk*.

To stress test our portfolio, we can calculate what our finance costs would be at this higher rate and see how this impacts on our profitability. For Green Leaf Properties, if we ended up paying 5% p.a. instead of 3.3% p.a. our finance costs would increase from £7,164 to £11,000. The £11,000 is calculated as £220,000 × 5% = £11,000. Our profit before tax would fall from £5,162 to £1,326. So, the continued profitability of our property portfolio is heavily dependent on Green Leaf being able to refinance at a lower interest rate in the future.

Under this stress test, the interest cover for Green Leaf Properties would fall to £12,326 ÷ £11,000 = 1.12. Not much headroom.

(b) General rate increase

You could also apply this approach to stress test the profitability of your portfolio and the interest cover at a higher interest rate. For example, you could pick a higher interest rate of 7% p.a. and look at how this would impact on both the underlying profitability and the interest cover.

For Green Leaf Properties, an interest rate of 7% p.a. would push the business into a loss-making position and the interest cover would fall to less than 1. Not a great position to be in.

What can you do to manage this risk?

There are several things you can do to manage interest rate risk. You can opt for longer fixed-rate periods on your mortgages to fix your borrowing costs for five years or more. This will reduce your exposure to interest rate risk in the shorter term and it will also give you time to rebalance or adjust your portfolio, if needed. This is especially important if your interest cover is low.

Over the longer term, you can also decide to pay down some of your mortgage balances, e.g. to drop the LTV to 60% instead of 75% on a property. This might unlock a slightly lower interest rate too. The need to pay down mortgage balances to reduce interest rate risk and the desire to reinvest your profits in new rental properties will always be a source of tension in any decision making.

Finally, you could save up hard and pay off the mortgage balances for one or more of the properties in your portfolio. There are really no easy options here. This is a risk you'll have to monitor constantly and manage carefully over the longer term throughout your property investment journey.

(3) Revenue risk

Revenue risk is the risk that an event takes place which negatively impacts future business revenues.

For a property rental business, the principal revenue risk is a fall in market rents for one or more of your properties. This could happen because of specific risks relating to the property itself, e.g. a certain apartment block falls into disrepute or part of a town or city becomes unfashionable. Changes in economic conditions can also impact on market rents more widely.

Quantifying this risk

When it comes to quantifying revenue risk, we're better off sticking with a high-level sensitivity test. That is, we can look at the impact on profitability of a fall in market rents of a particular order. But how much of a fall would be sensible to model?

If we look to the 2007-2008 financial crisis as a test case, then rents in the worst affected areas of the UK fell at an annualised rate of 2-3% p.a. for 12 to 18 months over the course of 2010 to 2011 as the economy suffered. After this, rents started to rise again.

Based on this, a reasonable stress test to model could be a 5% fall in revenues. For Green Leaf Properties, based on a revenue figure of £21,600, a 5% fall would mean a drop in revenues of £1,080 i.e. £21,600 × 5%. Profits would fall too, but by a slightly lower amount, as our management fees, which are set as a percentage of the rent collected, would likely also fall if rents were reduced.

Depending on your views about the general economy or how the properties in your portfolio would fare in a recession, you could choose to model a more pessimistic scenario than this. For example, you could model the impact of a 10% fall in rents.

What can you do to manage this risk?

The rental market in any economy tends to be a fragmented one. Even in a recession, there will be parts of the country where rents continue to rise due to local supply and demand factors. On the flip side, even in boom times, there will be certain towns, cities or even streets, that fall out of favour and where rents fall.

Your biggest enemy here is concentration risk. That is, if all your rental properties are located in a single area, the profitability of your portfolio will live and die by the fortunes of this one area. The antidote to this particular poison is diversification. So, unless you're wedded to a particular area, e.g. if you manage the properties yourself, it should be part of your strategy to diversify your portfolio across a range of towns and cities. You should also aim to invest in a range of different property types, e.g. flats versus houses.

Diversification will help to make your portfolio more robust and restrict revenue falls to within manageable bounds.

(4) Expense risk

Expense risk is the risk that the expenses associated with running your business increase. In turn, this will decrease the profitability of your business and could push you into a loss-making position.

For a property rental business, the principal expenses (other than finance costs which we covered above) are ground rents and service costs, management fees, marketing costs, repairs and insurance premiums. We discussed these at length in previous chapters.

When it comes to quantifying this risk, we're better off sticking with a high-level stress test, as we did for revenue risk. That is, we could model the impact on profitability of an across-the-board increase of 5% or 10% in all our expenses.

For Green Leaf Properties, the sum of our cost of sales of £6,720 and our administration expenses of £2,554 gives a total of £9,274 for expenses, excluding finance costs. Therefore, a 5% increase in our expense base would reduce our profits by £464.

We discussed at length in a previous chapter how you can go about managing these costs and the levers you can pull to improve performance. However, there's little you can do to avoid this risk or transfer it to a third party via insurance. Your best weapon against expense risk is to be conservative in your modelling before you buy a property to make sure there's enough cash flow and a large enough margin for safety in the deal.

Ultimately, if there's really nothing you can do to reduce expenses further, your best strategy might be to cut your losses and sell an underperforming property. This can free up your funds to invest in better deals elsewhere.

(5) Model risk

Finally, I just want to say a quick word on model risk. Model risk is the risk that a financial model that we're using fails or performs inadequately. This can lead to adverse outcomes for the business.

For a property rental business, the main risk is that the financial model we use to assess a potential deal and the due diligence we perform leads to an overly optimistic estimate of the profitability of a future investment. If we underestimate the expenses or overestimate the market rent, then our investment will perform much worse than expected. Over the long term, a series of bad deals has the potential to kill your property portfolio. So, remember, making a bad deal is worse than making no deal at all.

Our best protection against model risk is to make sure the figures we're using in our models are based on thorough research. And, if it's not possible to get the information we need for our model, then we should be conservative with our estimates.

Other risks to think about

In addition to the risks we've discussed so far, there are a variety of other risks you might want to think about.

- Operational risk – The risk of losses due to poor systems and procedures is something every business must contend with. For a property rental business, this would cover everything from fraud to tenant lawsuits. The risks you're running will vary for each business and need to be managed accordingly. Also, make sure to use insurance where it's needed.

- Regulatory risk – This is the risk that changes in regulations or legislation will affect your business. This is a key risk for property rental businesses, as the environment is constantly evolving. There will inevitably be changes to tenancy laws and regulations, health and safety standards and to the tax system. To stay on top of these, make sure you take the right advice.

As the size of your portfolio grows, the level of risk management you need to apply will likely increase. So, make sure to take advice and to grow a strong team around you who can help with this. When it comes to risk management, using the experience of your team is key to being successful. If you've never invested through a financial crisis before, it can help to speak to someone who has. Likewise, if you've never had to evict a tenant before, make sure to get some help with this.

A word or two on inflation risk

You may be wondering why I've not talked about inflation risk at all in this chapter. That's because the impact of inflation is not an easy risk to discuss. In general, higher inflation can have a positive impact on your returns. As we saw in the chapter on financing, property prices tend to increase in line with inflation over the long term. This, coupled with the impact of leverage, can lead to strong total returns over the long term in an inflationary world. However, the short-to-medium term impacts of inflation are often more difficult to see.

A simple thought experiment

Suppose we have a rental property in our portfolio which generates £9,000 of revenue per year. In addition, the cost of sales is around £3,000 and the finance costs are around £3,000. Our annual profit from this property would be £9,000 – £3,000 – £3,000 = £3,000. Our profit per month would be £250.

If inflation picks up and runs at 10% p.a. for five years, then property prices could well increase over this period, but we've not yet sold the property, so we have not realised any gains at this point. At this point, we're more concerned with our rental profits.

Let's try a little thought experiment to estimate the potential impact of this scenario on profitability. Suppose our rental income and revenue keeps pace with inflation over these five years. This isn't always true, as wages and salaries and (consequently) increases in rents often lag general price inflation, but we're going to be generous and assume that rents have kept pace. In this case, revenue will have increase to £9,000 × 1.10^5 = £14,495.

Our cost of sales will likely also have increased in line with inflation. I'll estimate this as £3,000 × 1.10^5 = £4,832.

But here comes the kicker

In a world where inflation is running at 10% each year, central banks will likely have increased interest rates to get the inflation rate under control. They'll increase interest rates to discourage borrowing and encourage saving, thereby reducing the general demand for goods and services in an economy. If you came off your five-year fixed rate mortgage at this time, the base rate might be up at the 8% level and buy-to-let mortgage rates up at say 10%. If the £3,000 per annum finance cost in our example was based on an interest rate of 3.3%, then our new finance cost after re-mortgaging at 10% could be £9,000 or so. The table below then, shows how the profitability of our investment could look before and after.

Impact of inflationary environment on profitability

£	Before	Impact	After
Revenue	9,000	× 1.10^5	14,495
Cost of sales	(3,000)	× 1.10^5	(4,832)
Finance costs	(3,000)	× (10% ÷ 3.3%)	(9,000)
Profit/(loss)	3,000		663
Profit per month	250		55

Overall, therefore, we would estimate the revised profitability on this property after five years as follows. Revenue of £14,495 – £4,832 cost of sales – £9,000 in finance costs. Our revised profit would be £663 for the year or just £55 per month. That is, our rental profits have been eroded considerably over the medium term by the impact of the higher interest rates brought on by this bout of inflation.

At this point, our best strategy for restoring the profitability of our portfolio might be to sell a couple of the properties in our portfolio and use any gains realised to pay down the mortgage balances on our other properties, so there are ways out of this conundrum.

Looking even further out

If we project things further out in the example above, then our revenues and cost of sales might continue to rise in line with inflation. If our finance costs stayed the same or fell longer term, e.g. if the inflation rate is brought under control and interest rates are lowered again, then the profitability of our portfolio is likely to be restored. In addition, if we haven't sold any of our properties and if we're sat on some large capital gains, then we're likely to be back in a healthy position again.

I've introduced this example to illustrate that whilst inflation risk is generally a positive one for property investors, inflation can and does bring its own risks to profitability over the short-to-medium term that need to be managed. In my view, there's not enough discussion on this in the property world, so I hope this simple example serves as an illustration of the potential risks.

In addition, property investors also need to think about and manage the risks associated with negative inflation or deflation.

This is a complicated topic and one which needs careful thought. To really understand the risks here you need to become a student of history and look back to both previous financial crises and major economic shocks to think about how these risks might play out over the short, medium and long term.

In conclusion

That brings us to the end of our chapter on risk management for property investors. Risk management is a vast topic. Experts in the field have dedicated their whole lives to developing frameworks and models that can be used to assess and manage risks for all kinds of businesses. As such, what we've covered in this chapter is just a first taste to whet your appetite.

Before I wrap this up, I did want to include one final comment on scenario testing. In the analysis above, we mainly looked at the impact of these risks in isolation. In practice, however, nothing happens in isolation. For example, a fall in market rents could well be accompanied by a fall in interest rates in a recession. Central banks would likely lower interest rates to try to get the economy moving again. As such, you may want to include some scenario testing in your risk analysis as well.

What is scenario testing?

In scenario testing, we consider the impact of complete scenarios, each with their own narrative. That is, we look at the impact of a specific combination of variables. Let me explain.

Modelling the Great Depression

In the Great Depression between 1930 and 1933, the following combination of macroeconomic variables played out in the US:

- the employment rate rose from 9% to 25%
- prices fell by around 20-25% in just four years
- interest rates were held low at between 0.5% and 1.4%

If you were to model the impact of a Great Depression type scenario, you might assume a base rate of 1% and buy-to-let mortgage rates of 3% or so. Likewise, you could assume tenant default rates of say 30% and a fall in both market rents and expenses of around 20%.

An inflationary oil shock scenario

Another scenario you could consider is the inflationary oil shock of the 1970s. Over the ten-year period from 1970, the US saw the following combination of macroeconomic variables:

- unemployment rates of between 5% and 10%
- prices increased by between 3% and 12% each year
- interest rates fluctuated between 4% and 11%

In your scenario analysis, you might assume a base rate of say 8% and buy-to-let mortgage rates of 10% or so. In addition, you could assume tenant defaults of say 20% and an increase in market rents and expenses of say 60% over 10 years.

I've picked off some economic scenarios here from US historical data, as this data was easily accessible online. But you could develop you own scenarios, based on historical economic data for the UK.

What we are trying to do here is develop some economic scenarios that can test the resilience of our portfolio under a variety of future shocks. And if you don't like the results you get, you might consider making some structural changes to your property portfolio to address these exposures.

Scenario analysis is another tool in the investors' toolkit to help with risk management. You can use it, or not – it's up to you. You'll likely find it more meaningful if the scenarios you use in your modelling are based on your view of the future and on what you think is likely to happen in practice.

Chapter 10

Golden rules of portfolio building

What the wise man does in the beginning, the fool does in the end.

–Howard Marks, *Mastering the Market Cycle*

This last chapter is all about how to use the property cycle to build your portfolio over the longer term. The property cycle itself is one of the most misused ideas in property investment. Many people have heard of the cycle, but lots of the discussions around it are either overly simplistic or overly definitive. Many pundits use the cycle predictively to express grand views about how the cycle will play out in the future. This often includes giving down-to-the-year style crystal ball predictions about when the market will peak. Similarly, they like to guess at when the next crash will come. I'm going to try to set the record straight a little here.

Once we've run through the basics of the property cycle, we'll look at how to use it to build your portfolio. And I'll give you my golden rules for portfolio building.

In the first section, I'm going to borrow from ideas put forward by the famous distressed-debt investor Howard Marks. In his excellent book, Mastering the Market Cycle, Marks shares his insights on the topic of market cycles. He covers topics like the economic cycle, the credit cycle, and the real estate cycle. He talks about how to position yourself at various points in the cycle and how the best we can really hope for is to tip the odds in our favour, as no-one really knows how the future will play out. It's well worth a read. I'm going to piggyback off the ideas in his book and look at how we can use these insights to our advantage in property investment.

What is the property cycle?

The property cycle is a sequence of recurrent events, a pattern if you will, that plays out across property markets. Like other investments, property tends to follow a predictable cycle. The cycle itself has four different phases. I'm going to talk you through the flavour of each of these phases with a sort of market commentary on what typically happens at each stage in the cycle.

The recovery phase

Let's start out with the recovery phase. At the beginning of this phase, prices have just fallen in a recent market crash. Prices have in fact fallen to a level where yields are high and the monthly cash flows are strong. This is because prices have fallen much more than rents. For contrarian investors with cash resources to spare, this is a fantastic time to be buying.

At this point in the cycle, there will be very few buyers in the market. The average investor has been badly burned in the last crash and is still licking their wounds. They may have sold at the bottom and crystallised large losses. The media will be downbeat, even though the worst of the recession appears to be over and property prices have stabilised somewhat.

As rents and cash flows start to increase and as brave investors lend support to prices, the recovery phase starts to develop. More and more buyers acquire the confidence to re-enter the market. Property prices start to rise. This happens in the prime locations first, with early price growth being mainly in the big cities and city centre hotspots. Then it starts to ripple out.

The boom phase

With the recovery gathering pace, the market will gradually move into the explosive boom phase. At the start of the boom, it will now be clear that prices are increasing. More investors will return to the market. The banks have now repaired their balance sheets and they are keen to lend again. This will provide a boost to the market as cheap-and-easy financing increases.

House prices start to increase at a much faster pace. Prime cities and city centre locations will switch into another gear and unloved secondary locations will start to see their first price rises. Better times and an improved economic backdrop will make providers of capital more optimistic. Banks will start to forget the lessons of the last crash and financing becomes easier still.

Now we're well into the boom phase. Yields have fallen, and higher property prices have made deal cash flows less attractive, except perhaps in secondary locations. Savvy investors are struggling to make property deals work. They can't find value anywhere, so they stop striking deals. They might even sell a property or two to lock-in their gains, but no-one will pay attention to this. The public, however, encouraged by the recent price rises, begin to speculate on property investments. Property TV shows are all over the airwaves.

The mania phase

At a certain point, logic appears to leave the market and groupthink takes over. We're now entering the mania phase. Banks have relaxed their lending criteria as far as they can go, and credit standards are what can only be described as lax. The higher prices go, the more everyone believes they will continue to do so. The vast amount of money pouring into the market keeps prices going up and up.

We're now into the last couple of years of the explosive boom phase. This is often called the winner's curse – if you're the last person to buy at the peak of the market, then you're the one who will take the hit in the next crash, which is now just around the corner.

The crash or slump phase

Just before the crash, the market is driven purely by sentiment, rather than fundamentals. At some point, confidence starts to dip a little. The banks begin to look at their ballooning loan books and worry about whether some of these loans will ever be repaid. Financing suddenly dries up – almost overnight it seems. Confidence evaporates completely, taking the market with it.

Property prices start to plummet. Individuals and investors who are over-leveraged go bankrupt. This triggers a wave of repossessions and forced property sales which add to the downward pressure on prices. The media stokes the fire with lots of bad news headlines. And speculators who bought at the peak in negative cash flow positions sell up, crystallising their losses.

After a year or two of falling prices and bad economic data, we start to see the first green shoots of recovery. Unemployment peaks and rents stop falling. Brave investors start to look at deals again.

To their surprise, some of the deals start to look attractive. If only they could raise the capital to invest. The odd bank agrees to start lending again, albeit their financing terms are tougher. Investors are asked to put in 40% or more of the purchase price themselves, that is a 60% LTV mortgage. The recovery phase starts to get underway, and the whole cycle starts again.

The missing piece of the puzzle

In the narrative above, I've described how elements such as investor psychology, attitudes to risk, and the availability of financing feed into the property cycle. These are all elements most financial cycles have in common, including the property cycle. But the property cycle incorporates one other ingredient that other financial cycles don't share – long lead times.

In the property market, there can be significant lead times before a new building comes on to the market to meet additional demand. Developers need to carry out economic feasibility studies. They need to find and purchase a new piece of land or development site. The building has to be designed, planning permissions have to be granted, and financing has to be secured. And all this needs to take place before developers can put a spade in the ground to start construction. All in all, the property development process can take years. For a major project, the whole process can take more than a decade from start to finish.

How long lead times impact the property cycle

To see how long lead times interact with the other factors discussed, let's look at the following short description of the property cycle from Howard Marks in

Mastering the Market Cycle. I have included his description of the property cycle verbatim.

- Bad times cause both the level of building activity to be low and the availability of capital for building to be constrained.
- In a while the times become less bad, and eventually good.
- Better economic times cause the demand for premises to rise.
- With few buildings having been started during the soft period and now coming on stream, this additional demand for space causes the supply/demand picture to tighten and thus rents and sales prices to rise.
- This improves the economics of real estate ownership, reawakening developers' eagerness to build.
- The better times and improved economics also make providers of capital more optimistic. Their improved state of mind causes financing to become more readily available.
- Cheaper, easier financing raises the pro forma returns on projects, adding to their attractiveness and increasing developers' desire to pursue them.
- Higher projected returns, more-optimistic developers and more-generous providers of capital combine for a ramp-up in building starts.
- The first completed projects encounter strong pent-up demand. They lease up or sell out quickly, giving their developers good returns.
- These good returns – plus each day's increasingly positive headlines – cause still more buildings to be planned, financed and green-lighted.
- Cranes fill the sky (and additional cranes are ordered from the factory, but that's a difference cycle). It takes years for the buildings started later to reach completion. In the interim, the first ones open eat into the unmet demand.
- The period between the start of planning and the opening of a building is often long enough for the economy to transition from boom to bust. Projects started in good times often open in bad times, meaning their space adds to vacancies, putting downward pressure on rents and sale prices. Unfilled space hangs over the market.
- Bad times cause the level of building activity to be low and the availability of capital for building to be constrained.

From this description, we can see that the last point in the list is the one that kicks off the next iteration. In this way, such cycles are self-perpetuating.

How long is a typically property cycle?

Long lead times in the development process are then a major driver on the supply side and influence the length of a typical property cycle. Property cycles can last anywhere between 15 and 25 years from peak to peak or from crash to crash. And the property cycle can interact with other cycles in the wider economy.

The important thing to remember is that property prices increase in line with inflation or higher over the long term. But the cycle means these price increases don't happen in a linear fashion. Prices will increase faster in the boom phase and they will fall or stagnate in the crash or slump phase. But the overall trend is generally upwards and in line with inflation.

Spotting where we are in the cycle

We can get some clues on where we are in the cycle by looking at the things going on around us.

For example, in the recovery, we'll have recently experienced a fall in prices and property will be out-of-favour. Plenty of people will likely still be in negative equity, and the press headlines on property will be downbeat. Financing will be hard to get, but the odd lender may have returned to the market. Building projects started in the boom will be left unfinished, but the odd brave developer might take on one of these projects as a repossession. As activity starts to pick up, prices start to rise a little.

In the boom phase, the lenders will be lending, and the builders will be building. People will have forgotten the pain of the last crash and property will be attracting headlines as prices are soaring. Lots of new building projects will be started and cranes will fill the skyline. In the final years of the boom, the media will be blurting out all kinds of nonsense. Financing will be cheap and easy. Massive vanity projects like huge skyscrapers will be announced. Property prices will make no sense. It will feel like a bubble, because it is one.

Then comes the crash or market slump. No description is needed. Trust me, you'll know when you're in a crash.

How to use the property cycle

In the final section of this chapter, I'm going to look at how to use the property cycle to build your property portfolio.

I'm going to give you my five golden rules of portfolio building. Some of these will sound so obvious you may question their usefulness. However, one of the hardest things to do over the long term is to keep your investment focus crystal clear and to keep your head when others are losing theirs. I hope you will use these golden rules as a filter for every property deal you make in the future.

Golden rules of portfolio building

Golden rule # 1 – Only invest in properties that provide cash flow

We've covered this rule in detail in Chapter 2, but it really is the most important rule of property investing. If a property doesn't provide you with a monthly cash, preferably one with a good margin for safety, then you shouldn't be doing the deal.

When it comes to the property cycle, the best time to be buying from a cash flow perspective is in the recovery phase and at the start of the boom. Later on in the cycle, yields will have fallen, and cash flow will be hard to find. That doesn't mean you shouldn't be investing at all later in the cycle, but it does mean you'll likely have a much harder time striking good deals.

If you follow this rule diligently, it'll mean being more aggressive and ramping up your investing activities when cash flows are at their strongest in the early part of the cycle. It'll also mean holding back and refraining from making bad deals later in the cycle.

Golden rule # 2 – Use the ripple effect to your advantage

Predicting which areas and which properties will experience strong capital growth in the future is a really difficult thing to do. The best tool in the property investor's tool kit is to try to take advantage of the ripple effect in some way.

As we saw in the above descriptions, different towns and cities experience their growth at different points in the cycle. Let's take the 2007-2008 financial crisis for instance. After falling to a low in 2009, property prices rebounded in London. First, we saw growth in the prime areas of central London, then price increases rippled out to the surrounding areas. It took several years before prices in Leeds started to rise. Between 2014 and 2018, however, prime properties in the city centre of Leeds experienced strong growth, but properties located on the outskirts of town have yet to experience the same level of growth.

Let's try to generalise this rule slightly. Early in the cycle, properties in prime cities and prime locations will likely experience the first bout of capital growth. This growth will start to make properties slightly further out look comparatively cheaper, and so this price growth will start to ripple out. To take advantage of the ripple effect, you need to buy in the right location at the right time. You'll need to study how prices are increasing in different towns and cities at various points in the cycle and try to get in ahead of the trend.

Another way to use the ripple effect is to invest in areas which are set to receive big investment. This could, for example, mean city centre regeneration projects to revitalise an unloved part of town. It could also mean big infrastructure projects like HS2.

Golden rule # 3 – Manage your leverage carefully

Our golden rule number three is to manage your leverage carefully. We've talked about how to quantify the risks relating to leverage in our previous chapter, so we won't cover that again here. But we will think about what this means during the cycle.

If you have bought well during the recovery phase and used the ripple effect to your advantage, you may well have experienced some strong capital growth by the later part of the cycle. At this point, you might be tempted to re-mortgage one or more of your properties at a higher LTV and pull some of your capital out, thereby allowing you to re-invest and expand your portfolio.

If you do decide to re-mortgage, make sure you properly model the impact on cash flows (see Golden rule # 1). The increase in borrowing will increase your finance costs, which will reduce your cash flow. As such, you should do this only if the property has experienced strong price growth *and* an increase in cash flow due to an increase in the market rent.

Some investors, I'm one of them in fact, like to keep a number of unencumbered properties in their portfolio. Having properties without mortgages on them means you'll have a stronger monthly cash flow to ride out any dip in market rents or an increase in interest rates. You'll also have a strategic asset you can sell or mortgage if you suddenly need a chunk of cash quickly.

Being over-leveraged is the biggest risk for property investors – make sure you manage this risk carefully.

Golden rule # 4 – Avoid the winner's curse

The last couple of years of the boom period are known as the winner's curse. Avoid the winner's curse like the plague. That is, don't buy any new properties and don't re-finance. Use this time to get ready for the coming crash. It's as simple as that.

Golden rule # 5 – Build a tactical cash buffer before the slump

We've all heard the Warren Buffett quote 'we simply attempt to be fearful when others are greedy and to be greedy only when others are fearful'. Well, Golden rule # 4 covers the first part, but what about the second bit of this mantra?

To take advantage of a market crash or slump, we need to build up our resources during the boom phase to take advantage of the crash. You should aim to build as big a cash buffer as you can in the years before the slump. If you've stopped doing deals and your monthly cash flows are strong, then this should be do-able.

Likewise, if you've kept a couple of properties unencumbered, there could be some creative things you can do on the financing side to secure the lending you need. For example, allow a lender to take a mortgage charge on an unencumbered property.

Managing your emotions will be key here. You'll feel like you're missing out on the end of the boom phase and that you could be putting that spare cash to better use. Don't. Stayed disciplined and you'll be thankful for it later.

In conclusion

The property cycle is one of the most powerful concepts in property investing. Knowing about the cycle will help you to make sense of things when others are confused about the direction of the market. It will give you the confidence you need to fight against the tide and manage your emotions. After all, managing your emotions is half the battle when it comes to investing.

Conclusion

That brings us to the end of our journey. You're now armed with all the essential property investment calculations you need to know to take your property investing to the next level. You can feel confident in your knowledge that there's no hidden secrets or magic formulae you're missing out on. You can feel excited about the fact that you are better equipped than 95% of property investors out there around how to assess deals and how to manage your portfolio.

However, before we part ways, I want to set out a challenge to anyone who's made it this far. And it's a challenge around systems and processes. The hard part about running a property portfolio isn't understanding the mathematical concepts or theoretical frameworks. The hard part is setting up your systems and processes in a way that ensures you use this knowledge day-in and day-out to maximise the returns you make. You need to be disciplined in the way you assess, stress test, and negotiate deals. And you need to be disciplined in your approach to evaluating the return on your investments, managing the risks in your portfolio, and building your portfolio over time. This discipline is what separates average investors from professionals, and it's what will take your property investment to the next level.

I hope that you've enjoyed the book and that you are feeling confident about the journey ahead. The skills and techniques you've learned in this book are only the start, the rest you'll learn in the doing. When it comes to investment, there really is no substitute for experience. If you're interested in the free resources I've put together to accompany the book, make sure to register for those. You'll find details of how to do so in the pages which follow. Otherwise, I'll leave it here for now. Thanks for reading, and best of luck with your future endeavours.

Glossary

Base rate – The rate of interest the Bank of England charges on lending to banks.

Capital employed – The sum of owners' equity and debt liabilities; can be calculated as Total Assets less Current Liabilities.

Ground rent – The annual charge levied by the freeholder on the leaseholder.

Land registry – A government office which is responsible for holding records of land ownership and any charges, including mortgages, against the property.

Lease – The legal document governing the occupation by the tenant of a premises for a specific length of time. At the period end, the property reverts to the owner.

Loan to value (LTV) – The ratio of the mortgage to the value of the property, e.g. if you borrow £75,000 to purchase a house worth £100,000, the LTV is 75%.

Negative equity – When the property is worth less than the outstanding mortgage.

Return on capital employed (ROCE) – Shows how well a company is using both its equity and debt to generate a return.

Return on equity (ROE) – Return on equity shows the return earned by the owners of the business after all expenses relating to debt and borrowings have been paid.

References

1. Shiller, R. (2016). *Irrational Exuberance: Revised and Expanded Third Edition.* Princeton University Press.
2. Kiyosaki, R. (2017). *Rich Dad Poor Dad: What the Rich Teach Their Kids About Money That the Poor and Middle Class Do Not!* Plata Publishing.
3. Graham, B. (2003). *Intelligent Investor: The Definitive Book on Value Investing - A Book of Practical Counsel.* Harper Business.
4. Isaac, D., O'Leary, J. (2012). *Property Valuation Principles.* Red Globe Press.
5. Taleb, N. (2013). *Antifragile: Things that Gain from Disorder.* Penguin.
6. Voss, C., Raz, T. (2017). *Never Split the Difference: Negotiating as if Your Life Depended on It.* Random House Business.
7. Cialdini, R. (2007). *Influence: The Psychology of Persuasion.* Harper Business.
8. Drucker, P. (200). *The Practice of Management.* Routledge.
9. McElroy, K. (2015). *The ABCs of Property Management: What You Need to Know to Maximize Your Money Now.* RDA Press LLC.
10. Marks, H. (2020). *Mastering the Market Cycle: Getting the odds on your side.* Nicholas Brealey Publishing

Get the free resources

I've prepared some free resources to accompany the material in this book. All you need to do to access them is register for free on my website. These resources include the following:

- my spreadsheet for assessing property deals
- my spreadsheet for modelling a property refurbishment
- a one-page summary of all the key calculations

The spreadsheets are the ones I use myself for assessing buy-to-let property deals. It's all completely free with no sell on. Just sign up at my website at:

www.essentialproperty.net/free-resources